Get Your Life Back is .... command from the heart of the heavenly Father. This book will challenge you to take an active role in your process to freedom. In this one of a kind book, Floyd A. Walters Jr. provides a candid look at the cause and effects of bitterness. Using personal experience and revelations to equip you to eradicate the root of bitterness and live life forward. Floyd is a man of wisdom and integrity with a passion to empower people to fulfill their destiny. He is a mighty man of valor, with a heart of righteousness. I have personally witnessed his resolve and determination to live a life free from bitterness. He is a man who lives what he preaches. This book is a valuable resource that I highly recommend.

—MICHELLE McCLAIN-WALTERS
AUTHOR, *THE PROPHETIC ADVANTAGE* AND
THE ESTHER ANOINTING
CHICAGO, IL

In the years that I have known Floyd Walters, I have never seen his face light up as when he became to discuss *Get Your Life Back*. It is clear that God has given him insight into this important subject in which so many people battle. Not only does Floyd help you to recognize the roots of bitterness, but he also gives clear solutions to bring the reader to freedom. I would strongly recommend this book to anyone who has struggled with hurt or offense. You will receive answers. This book can be an important resource for those who minister to people or who have friends who are dealing with bitterness. You will find keys to open those doors.

—APOSTLE MICHAEL POSEY
SENIOR LEADER, CHURCH OF THE HARVEST

I have known Pastor Floyd for many years, and I have seen the dignity, humility, and strength of character of this general. His journey began from the ranks of a seemingly low place. His book, *Get Your Life Back*, chronicles some of the vast wisdom and experience he has amassed in his incredible journey of life.

You will learn that bitterness is a killer! It kills your relationship with God, your relationship with others, your potential, and your future. If you do not forgive and release it out of your heart and life, you won't be able to flourish and fulfill your potential by advancing the kingdom of God.

So, I am recommending to all that they don't only read and study this book but also to recommend it to others. The wisdom, insight, grace, and anointing on this book will help you to be delivered from bitterness and help you fulfill your purpose in the earth.

—APOSTLE JAMES DUNCAN
SENIOR PASTOR, CHRIST CHURCH INTERNATIONAL INC.
BROOKLYN, NY

I've known Floyd for several years and during that time, he proven himself to be a man of integrity and a man who loves God. His new book, *Get Your Life Back*, confronts the topic of bitterness, a condition that many are living with daily. As a result of what Floyd has suffered, he has gained much wisdom. This insight on divine strategies reveal how to confront bitterness and eradicate the spirit of bitterness. I strongly recommend this book, and I implore any person who reads this book to apply the strategies found within. I believe this book will help many to finally become free of bitterness and live an offense-free life.

—APOSTLE ALVIN GREEN
OVERSEER/SENIOR APOSTLE,
WORLD HARVEST MINISTRIES
COLUMBIA, SC

Get **your** Life Back

Get **Your** Life Back

Floyd A. Walters Jr.

Visit the author's website at: www.floydwaltersministries.com

International Standard Book Number: 978-0-9993544-0-7
E-book ISBN: 978-0-9993544-1-4

First edition

17 18 19 20 21 — 987654321
Printed in the United States of America

I firmly believe God is all-knowing. With this understanding, He's aware of what each person needs to release their potential and walk in their destiny. Being in a fertile environment along with being in covenant with godly people is critical to a person's success and happiness. My wife is that person who constantly encourages and endorses me, and speaks life back into me.

I've learned plenty from my wife, who is an accomplished author herself. She is the author of several books namely The Prophetic Advantage, The Esther Anointing, The Deborah Anointing, *and others. I have seen her tenacity and commitment to completing her books. I have gleaned much strength and admiration from watching her dedication to her craft. It is with great pleasure that I dedicate this book to my loving wife, Michelle McClain-Walters.*

I am also dedicating this book to my only son, Jeremiah Nicholas Walters.

Son, when I looked into your face I saw myself. I saw the striking resemblance, an innocence in your face but also a sadness in your eyes. When I looked at you, you always brought me joy and drove me to always want to be a godly example for you. From the day you were born, you were my little God-man. Son, I was very sad about your passing so soon, but our heavenly Father assured me you are safe in His presence.

I pray this book will help many people to deal with life's pains, hurts, and bitterness in a productive manner. I dedicate this book, my ministry, and the church to your memory. I love you forever.

CONTENTS

FOREWORD

THIS BOOK WILL help those who have suffered from painful relationships and the resulting hurt and bitterness that often follow. There are many who cannot go into their future because they are carrying unresolved hurts and wounds from the past. Floyd Walters has done an excellent job in explaining from the Word of God and personal experience the solutions to what multitudes suffer from every day.

There are so many people in need of deliverance and healing. Betrayal. hurt, abuse, and rejection has marred the lives of many. These are spiritual problems that need spiritual solutions. We have learned a great deal in the past years concerning deliverance from these issues, and we are constantly learning new truths to add to our understanding. Many authors are helping us to understand more fully how to come out of unresolved issues, and receive healing.

Floyd Walters gives wisdom in dealing with issues that destroy many lives. Wisdom is the principal thing. It takes godly wisdom to be able to come out of bondage and repair the broken areas of your life. God is a God of restoration and healing. We must look to Him as our Great Physician, and trust His wisdom to receive restoration. We must confront these issues in a godly way and learn the truths that will help us out of sometimes horrible situations.

I also believe God wants those who learn these truths to teach others. We can be able ministers if we have knowledge and wisdom. This book contains a wealth of wisdom that will not only help those in need but prepare them to teach others as well.

God has a plan and purpose for every person. Satan is a thief and destroyer. Don't allow the enemy to use hurt, abandonment, and betrayal to abort God's plan for your life. Learn to come out of any bitterness that would poison your life. Let any root of bitterness be but cut out of your life and receive total freedom and deliverance.

I know Floyd Walters's personal journey as well. He has had to overcome challenges in his personal life. He uses his challenges, and resulting victories, as a testimony of God's power to heal and deliver. He is speaking from experience in this book. His experiences and victory will stir you to be an overcomer as well. I trust that the words and teachings in this book will bless you and encourage you. Allow the teaching and testimony in this book to shatter any hurt, pain, or bitterness in your life. You are an overcomer.

—JOHN ECKHARDT
APOSTLE, CRUSADERS CHURCH AND IMPACT NETWORK
BEST-SELLING AUTHOR, *PRAYERS THAT ROUT DEMONS*
CHICAGO, IL

ACKNOWLEDGMENTS

I WOULD FIRST LIKE to acknowledge my Lord and Savior Jesus Christ, who freed me from a life of sin and confusion and who continues to transform my mind and awaken my spirit to the magnitude of His love that He has for me. I am eternally grateful for His favor and grace on my life. Lastly, I am grateful to Him for extending me the scribe's anointing to pen this book.

I would like to thank my college professors Geraldine Williams and Margaret Watts of Springfield College. These two women were the first people to encourage me to express myself through the written word. Professor Geraldine Williams was the first person to speak into my life and declared I would author a book someday.

I would like to acknowledge my pastor, Apostle John Eckhardt of Crusaders Church Chicago, IL. It was at his annual international Impact Conference in 2012, themed the Exponential Conference, that he released a writer's anointing for all would be authors. It was that endowment and released that I embraced that help me to write this book.

This book would not be completed without my acknowledging Regine Jean-Baptise, the founder of Go-Getter Enterprise. It was Ms. Jean-Baptise, that gave me the final push to go ahead and write this book. She was very instrumental in helping me organize this project. For her contribution, I am so ever grateful.

INTRODUCTION

Acrid bitterness inevitably seeps into the lives of people who harbor grudges and suppress anger, and bitterness is always a poison. It keeps your pain alive instead of letting you deal with it and get beyond it. Bitterness sentences you to relive the hurt over and over.
—LEE STROBEL[1]

VERYONE HAS EMOTIONS. They help us express how we feel. On their own, they are neither good nor bad. However, emotions left unchecked or unrestrained often have a negative consequence in a person's life. That negativity can control you! With this understanding, it is critical that people strive to maintain a firm grip on their emotions and a guard over their spirit. It is easy—and good—to embrace times of joy, but we must also be prepared to encounter some uncomfortable periods and events in the journey of life as well. If we are only equipped to process positive emotions, or if we develop a habit of filtering life's negative experiences through our senses based on how they look or sound alone, we potentially position ourselves to be poisoned and corrupted. The effect is often lasting and always damaging to the spirit.

There are many people living with wounded emotions and contaminated spirits because of traumatic events, injustices, life's trials, and ultimately, their own choices. Many believe these events were unfair. When this sense of injustice is coupled with prayers that don't seem to bring relief, they begin to believe God is no longer answering their cries. Harboring these feelings and beliefs is deadly.

Many people in and outside of the body of Christ are dying slowly because they have unknowingly succumbed to the grasp of the silent killer called the spirit of bitterness. This silent killer is a tormenting, imprisoning spirit that lives just below the surface of the person's frustration and pain. Its root system goes deep within a person's soul, where it eventually wraps its tentacles around the heart. This vicious, choking effect forces its prey to give the appearance and impression that everything is fine on the outside, while all along the victim lives a tormented and suffocating life. The victim is constantly forced to hold on to negative, painful memories and rehearse the trauma.

People worldwide experience trauma every day. It can take many forms: abandonment, abuse, assault, betrayal, physical harm, or even offense. When such an event occurs in someone's life, there is a critical moment when he or she develops a strategy for coping with that wound. At that moment, some choose to take up arms and fight to regain wholeness. Others choose, subconsciously, to allow their hurt to define them, and they become instantaneously a victim. They embrace feelings of unforgiveness and bitterness. The choice to harbor ill feelings toward their abuser without fully understanding the toxic residual effects that their decision will have on their own emotions, psyche, mind, body, and spiritual makeup is devastating and crippling to the embittered person. They may assume their hurt will end eventually, but instead it gets worse and worse.

There is an old adage that says time heals all wounds, but is that true? There are billions of people living today who have been offended, abandoned, abused, assaulted, betrayed, or otherwise physically wounded; they are the victims of horrendous crimes, some of which may have happened decades ago. But these same people are still reeling and suffering from their pain. Many are diagnosed as bipolar and taking medication like Prozac, Paxil, and Zoloft, just to name a few. All these medications have one thing in common: they do absolutely nothing to eradicate the bitter root that is lodged in their hearts. They only keep them in a medicated, synthetic high without solving the root of the problem. Drugs—both doctor-prescribed and illegal—create a mental and medical state that has the potential to turn the wounded person into a chemically dependent junkie.

But, glory to God, there is a way to loosen the grip of the silent killer. Every person has the right to live a life free of emotional and spiritual torment. I encourage you to reread the list of types of trauma in the previous paragraph. If you have experienced one or more of these wounds in your life—as nearly all of us have—it is time to allow the Holy Spirit to reveal to you if a root of bitterness is growing in your heart so that you can live in freedom and wholeness. This book will help you identify what bitterness is and how it can manifest. You will learn how to expose it in your own heart and how to help others identify its grasp. I will offer divine strategies and principles for uprooting and eradicating this demonic root—permanently—so that you and those you minister to can walk in your God-ordained fullness.

Are you ready to live the life God ordained for you? Are you prepared to help others experience wholeness? Let's get started.

Chapter 1

NAOMI'S STORY

IMAGINE THAT YOU are a woman living in a patriarchal society where you do not have a voice, a society where you are seen as a second-class citizen, and, in some cases, as a husband's property. This is a culture where a man, your husband, calls all the shots for the entire family. It is a culture where there is no vocational outlet for a woman, nor a chance of becoming educated. There are no shopping malls or coffee shops to frequent with friends; no hair salons or nail shops at which to congregate and rejuvenate; no cell phones, social media, or general media to connect her with the people and world around her and help her keep up with the latest trends or gossip. As a woman, your primary goal is to marry for support, safety, and sex. As a woman, you are subordinate to your husband in every way. And lastly, your greatest joy is to bear your husband a male child, because to have a son brought great honor on you as a woman and your husband.

In this patriarchal society, as with many ancient cultures, marriage was the ideal state. Parents arranged the marriages with the goal of finding a suitable match from the same tribe or belief system. The man was considered the head of the house. The woman was the helpmate. Women were to marry monogamously so that the identity of her children's father was always clear and the integrity of the father's lineage was guaranteed. Marriage was the norm for men and women. There was no notion to remain celibate in ancient Israel.

It is this cultural mind-set, entrenched and influenced by a male-dominated society, to which Naomi introduces us. Naomi was the wife of Elimelech. As a descendent of Nahshon and the daughter-in-law of Amminadab she was well connected to men of high standing in her community. It seems that her identity was wrapped up in who her father was, who her husband was, and her role as a wife and a mother.

Naomi and her husband found themselves living in a period when the judges ruled over Israel. It was a time when every man did what was right in his own eyes. It was a time of spiritual collapse, compromise, and apostasy.

To complicate matters, there was a severe famine in the land. The drought was strategic. It affected the people of the region, specifically—the rebellious followers of God. God used the famine as an instrument of discipline to bring about genuine repentance and a renewed commitment back to Him and His statutes. When there is a shortage of any kind, people tend to panic and become fearful. This spirit of fear creates in people's minds images of what might happen. These potential outcomes become an obsession, blinding the individual to their circumstances and forcing them to become shortsighted and leave genuine help. Often a lawless spirit is released. People begin to seek alternative ways of solving their dilemma and getting their needs meet without consulting God.

Naomi and her family found themselves in such a dilemma, even though her husband was a wealthy man. Elimelech was an Ephrathite of an ancient noble line. He was an influential man, a land owner, an aristocrat, a man whose name means "my God is King."[1] His name may suggest that he had a genuine relationship with God and that, that relationship was transformative. It may suggest that he placed honor on God and looked to Him for advice, direction, protection, and support. Nevertheless, while being given a powerful name at birth is prepossessing, living up to that name requires a decision to be made and a commitment to honor. The biblical record does not explicitly tell us about Elimelech's relationship with God, but we do know that when faced with famine and after taking a panoramic view of the crises happening around him, he shrunk down into a mental state of fear and foresaw himself as a beggar. In the time of famine, his wealth did not insulate or comfort him. He became fixated on his fear that he was not immune to the effects of the crisis.

We must ask the question, What drove him to leave Bethlehem Judah and go to the land of Moab? He was a wealthy man. He had the respect of the community. As an aristocrat and landowner, Elimelech was living large in a town where others were just getting by. After all, he was living in Bethlehem Judah, better known as the House of Bread. It was a place where people from the surrounding region were coming for sustenance, a place where God was still providing for him and his family! History had shown him that God would always provide for His covenant people. (See Genesis 22:14.) Despite this, Elimelech left for what he thought was a better place, maybe a haven for his family. Perhaps he could not imagine himself or his family standing in bread lines like beggars. Perhaps he could not imagine having to downsize and live on a lesser level. He could not imagine pinching pennies or asking for a handout.

It appears there was a spiritual famine in Elimelech's life before there was a physical famine. This was the case within the region and with the chosen people of God. When a believer's vertical relationship is out of order with God, his or her broken spiritual state threatens the unity and relationships within their home, community, church, and work. This gives birth to spirits of resentment and aids in fostering the spirit of bitterness. Elimelech failed the litmus test, not of acidy but of obedience and faith.

THE MOVE TO MOAB

Often when people move abruptly due to impending storms or famine, they travel somewhere relatively close.

They relocate to a familiar region where they know the people. Elimelech chose to find sanctuary in the land of Moab. The Moabite people were an enigma. They had a volatile, unstable relationship with foreigners, especially Israelites. Some historians believe the Moabite women led the Israelite men into sexual sin during the exodus and King Solomon into sin as king.[2] (See Numbers 25:1–2; 1 Kings 11:1, 7.) Nonetheless, it is here where Elimelech chose to move his family to what he believed was a safe place.

Who did he consult about the move to a place and people that were the natural enemy of his family, a people who had a different belief system and God? History does not tell us that he consulted his wife, Naomi. Would that even have been an option in such a male-dominated society? God said in His Word that He made man and wife one flesh (Gen. 2:21–24). That did not mean just physically but emotionally, spiritually, and intellectually. They were to be one flesh in every other way, including making life decisions. However, in ancient Israel the final decision was left up to the man. Did he even consider what she would be leaving and given up? Was Naomi in agreement with the move? Just maybe this was the beginning of Naomi's root of bitterness, but we will return to that later.

What might have been different if Elimelech had sought and listened to the word of the Lord on the matter? What did his family suffer because of non-compliance? Their relationships suffered, which started a downward spiral, a domino effect of trouble in their lives. Had Elimelech and his family remained in Bethlehem Judah, they would have remained under the canopy of God's protection, regardless of any crisis around them. Instead, a rash decision cost them physical and spiritual synergy with like, believing people. They lost their inherited land, their relatives, the church, their neighbors, and their position within the community.

A lesson must be learned here. Failure to acknowledge the God of the Bible with our decisions can result in negative consequences. It thrusts many people into seasons of suffering, heartache, and confusion. When we are driven by fear and pride, we find ourselves making the current crisis even worse with our rash and unwise decisions. Have you ever taken the time to trace back the origin of any of your life's troubles? Where did you make the wrong turn or decision?

When making life decisions, who do you consult? There is safety in the multitude of counsel (Prov. 11:14). As a safeguard or a preventive measure God implores believers, His followers, to acknowledge Him in all their ways (including decisions), and He promises to direct their path (Prov. 3:6). This is not to strip them of their independence but to help them become dependent on Him because an obedient lifestyle brings rewards (Isa. 1:19). Why does God want His followers to have such a mind-set? Simply to avoid trouble at all costs! The easiest way to avoid bitterness is staying in the counsel and will of God. When we do this we avoid the situations and attitudes that give the silent killer a foothold in our lives.

When tropical storms escalate into dangerous storms they are called hurricanes. Hurricane season occurs in the state of Florida. Now, there are categories of hurricanes that range in strength from dangerous (category 1) to catastrophic (category 5). As one may think, the higher the category number, the more dangerous the storm. When storms are predicted to range between category 4 and category 5, weather officials issue a stern warning to residents of the area to evacuate and move to a region that is not expected to be impacted by the deadly storm. Elimelech did not receive any such warning from officials or God about the famine instructing him to move to a safer environment. He just moved independently without God directing him and without receiving His approval. Now, there is nothing wrong with a man trying to protect his family or trying to ensure their safety, but this storm, this famine, was a result of God's people abandoning His statutes and living in open rebellion. By failing to heed the direction of the Lord, Elimelech stepped farther from God's favor.

PUTTING DOWN ROOTS

I'm sure the sojourn was supposed to be temporary, but after a period, Elimelech and his family began to assimilate into the culture and put down roots. They embraced their customs, their practices, and little by little the famine became a distant memory to them.

Elimelech and Naomi fathered two sons, Mahlon and Chilion. They grew and entrenched themselves into the Moabite society.

By moving to Moab, Elimelech had exposed his family to idol worship, child human sacrifice, a lifestyle of debauchery, and an ungodly value system, all because he thought it would be better in the land of Moab with plenty than in Bethlehem in lack. He removed his family from under the protective hand of God, from accountability partners and faithful friends. Without the accountability that a community of believers provides, people more easily expose themselves to unnecessary peril and conflict. What Elimelech and Naomi did not consider was that their rash decision would have long-lasting ramifications on their lives and their family.

Children repeat what they see their parents do more than avoid what they are told not to do. As a parent, I have witnessed this firsthand. Watching my kids celebrate similar victories, fighting some of the same battles, and maneuver around destructive landmines in life sometimes can take me down memory lane. But I know there are schemes to destroy their potential and plant seeds of doubt and worthlessness in their minds, schemes that will tempt them to conform to an eroding value system. It is through these various fiery darts of hate, economic injustice issues, and looking for affirmation in a chaotic world that we find the sons of Elimelech and Naomi.

At the height of the transition or judgement on Israel, while Mahlon and Chilion were still young, Elimelech was stricken, and he died suddenly. Being a follower of God is a great honor, but that distinction demands great accountability and responsibility on the disciple's part. Elimelech failed to uphold his end of the bargain when he left his home under precarious circumstances and against God's instructions. Behavior like this always comes with consequences, and for Elimelech it seems the consequence was death. We see this same principle in the life of Jonah, whose story is so familiar in our culture and whose attitude seems to parallel Elimelech's. Jonah did not want to partner with God and become His mouthpiece, nor assist in bringing salvation and deliverance to a dying people. Perhaps Jonah thought his disobedient behavior, his rebellious mind-set, somehow insulated him from impending divine discipline from the wrath of God. Perhaps he thought he was out of the reach of God and released from any responsibility for his chauvinistic and prideful attitude. Whatever he thought—and whatever Elimelech thought—God's sovereignty prevailed in both their lives. In spite of Jonah's negative attitude, God's plan to save the people of Nineveh prevailed; likewise, in spite of Elimelech's heritage as one of the people of God, his decision to step outside of His provision had fatal consequences. Jonah and Elimelech were both faced with the task of trusting in God's wisdom and obeying His directives, but both refused and suffered the consequences.

Naomi was surely left standing in the middle of the room stunned! Her husband, the man who gave her legitimacy, the man who provided her covering, the man people identified her with, was dead. Naomi was faced with the burden of burying her husband, the love of her life. She was alone with her children in a foreign land. She had no relatives to console her. Being an Israelite, it was hard for Naomi to make friends because of the racial tension that existed between her culture and that of the land in which she lived. Therefore, she only had casual relationships. There were no genuine girlfriends to weep and mourn with her. Naomi did not have access to a priest to pray over her deceased husband. There would not be anyone to eulogize the dead, nor words of comfort to ensure her that God was yet in control. Lastly, there were no mature family members around from which she could glean strength.

As Naomi raised her head, fixed her gaze on her two sons for strength, she saw Mahlon, whose name meant "weak, failing, pinning, sickly," and Chilion. I imagine that she may have discerned there was a lack of leadership qualities in her sons. She saw that there was an absence in her sons' makeup, and at that moment, within her mind, she prophesied doom and gloom for her future and theirs.

It was at this time, I imagine, that there was a knock at the door of Naomi's spirit. Perhaps at that moment, a confused and fearful Naomi allowed the silent killer into her world.

We all face the same choice when presented with trauma. When tragedy suddenly hit your life, how did you respond? Did you give in to the traumatic event and implode? Did you allow the silent killer into your situation, or did you rise like the phoenix? The Bible tells us our thought life will determine the course of our life and health. Proverbs 23:7 states that as a man thinks "in his heart, so is he." The person who adopts a pessimistic and hopeless attitude about their life and any current negative situation runs the risk of prophesying doom and gloom for the future. If you think positively, you will remain positive; however, if you think negatively about your circumstances, you will inevitably draw into your life the negativity you are dwelling on and create a space in which the root of bitterness can take hold—and take over.

After the death of Elimelech, Naomi was faced with the decision of whether or not to remain in that foreign land. She was left there with no genuine friends, no believers, and no property to call her own. Unfortunately, Naomi was a single mother for the first time as well. If she stayed, she would face the challenges of raising young men in an idolatrous and strange society. She would be forced to continue renting for years while supporting her sons. But, Naomi had another option. She could choose to leave that godless place and its negative influences on her and her sons.

I imagine that she paused and thought, "For the first time, I am able to call the shots!" No more hidden frustration and wishful thinking about if only she could have a say in any matter. Now she finally could!

God knows all the intimate details about us, but our adversary, the devil, studies us to learn us. He uses learned information about us and targets our areas of weakness. He is a strategist and only uses what works! The devil, working in tandem with the spirit of bitterness, targeted and exploited the weaknesses and unsurrendered areas of Naomi's life, thus solidifying her position to remain in Moab. This decision gave encouragement to the resentment lodging in her heart and endorsed the presence of the silent killer. It is here that Naomi yields, unknowingly, to demonic reasoning.

THE ROOTS TAKE HOLD

The Bible states that the devil understands bitterness. How? Because he was kicked out of heaven and lost his role as praise leader according to Isaiah 14:12–15. As a result, he understands bitterness very well, and he knows that it renders a person ineffective, steals their peace, and poisons their atmosphere.

Oftentimes, we crave a certain privilege, and when we are granted that new power it can become overwhelming and serve as a gateway to bondage. Before long, the newly found freedom in Naomi's life also brought newfound fear. She slipped into a state of depression and lost control over her sons. Instead of remaining loyal to the Israelite lifestyle, Mahlon and

Chilion married two Moabite women. There was no law expressly forbidden the marrying of the Moabite women, but it fell under the umbrella of what was off-limits for an Israelite. Deuteronomy 7:1–4 explicitly states that no such marriage between certain groups of people should take place:

> Neither shalt thou make marriages with them; thy daughter thou shalt not give unto his son, nor his daughter shalt thou take unto thy son. For they will turn away thy son from following me, that they may serve other gods: so will the anger of the LORD be kindled against you, and destroy thee suddenly.
>
> —DEUTERONOMY 7:3–4

You were not to give your sons and daughters to groups of people that were anti-God, but Elimelech had to have consented to these marriages. Perhaps he and Naomi made the arrangements before his death. God knew that children born from a union of compromise from His Law would ultimately disqualify them from true worship. This issue here is that marriage with someone who served other gods would create an unholy mixture in their children, which would inhibit them from going into the assembly of the Lord. Even to the tenth generation none of Elimelech's descendants could enter the assembly of the Lord "forever," according to Deuteronomy 23:3.

Many people draw negativity into their lives because

of ignorance or rebellion. The sons of Naomi demonstrated both when they chose to marry women who were not Israelites—and they reaped the consequences. They suffered from a spiritual dullness that endorsed their "What harm could this do?" mind-set. The Bible states in Song of Solomon 2:15 that it is "the little foxes, that spoil the vine." Those decisions that we think are insignificant or do not matter much often come back to haunt us.

This does not mean God is a tyrant, nor a despotic monarch; He is a loving God that only wants the best for mankind, which is why He provides guidelines in the Scriptures for us to follow. Parents understand that their children tend to go astray, so they put safety measures in place. God is no different. In His omniscience, He often protects His followers while allowing them to make their own decisions. He reserves the right to reprimand them and guide them back into safety. (See Hebrews 12:10–12.)

God foresaw Naomi's family coming out of Moab and returning to the house of faith. In order to avoid a transgenerational curse on Mahlon's and Chilion's unborn children, God, in His sovereignty, shut up the wombs of Orpah and Ruth, the young ladies married to Naomi's sons. The young women were probably nice, attractive young women from a good home. However, their upbringing in a pagan society, coupled with its anti-God value system, surely rubbed off on the boys.

Strange things change things. King Solomon went after foreign women, and it changed his heart toward God—and he was the wisest man who ever lived. He was somewhat of a connoisseur of strange women. Ask yourself the question, How many times did you covet something or someone, and a loved one tried to protect you from it? Nevertheless, with our ebullient temperament and strong will we go after it like a bull goes after the matador cape, not knowing the danger and death lies on the other side of that red cape. We all live in the aftermath of our decisions. We reap what we sow.

Naomi's sons were seemly caught up in these whirlwind romances, and like their father, they were suddenly stricken in the prime of their lives. Both died! Was it a curse or the result of disobedience? The Bible is clear in Leviticus 26 and Deuteronomy 28 that there is a promise of long life if we obey and a curse if we disobey. When unexplainable tragedies occur, many are at a loss for words. They try to find some type of reasoning for the tragedy, and if not found, they look for someone or something to blame. Sometimes the cause can be traced back to actions or behaviors that gave the enemy a foothold and prevented the Lord from intervening with blessing and protection.

Orpah and Ruth joined Naomi in the fraternity of widowhood. No doubt the girls had already suffered some short of ridicule for marrying Israelite men. They may have been ostracized or made the brunt of many jokes, and now they found themselves in emotional anguish and abandonment. Who would now want to marry such women? They went against culture and societal norms. How would they live? What kind of life could they expect to find? Would they even be welcome back into Moabite society? Would they become beggars, or even worse, prostitutes?

Their mother-in-law could not be of much help by this time. Naomi was on the verge of a mental breakdown. She unexpectedly buried her husband. And now her sons, her last line of defense for a supportive future, those who were supposed to make her a grandmother, were dead. Confusion, frustration, and bewilderment are likely what she was feeling. Naomi's only solace was the silent killer telling her, "It's alright to vent. It's alright to cuss. It's alright to blame somebody and embrace a grim outlook on life. It's alright to have resentment toward your deceased husband, God, and even yourself."

How do you make sense of a chaotic situation when you are consumed by its grasp? Chaotic situations can feel as if you're in a whirlwind vortex. Intense feelings can become intoxicating and magnetic as they slowly pull you toward bitterness. How do you remain sane? For the Christian, God often allows moments of clarity during trouble for the sole purpose of assessing our situation and drawing us back into His will. When we return to God, we must all ask the questions, What did I learn from the hard situation outside the will of God? Did I become wiser or dull of hearing? Did I become better instead of bitter? If you have examined your heart and have found you are already harboring bitterness, there is a way out. In fact, you are on the path to freedom right now! Just keep reading.

In the midst of the whirlwind around her, Naomi made the decision to return to Judah in search of family and in the hope of finding prosperity there. Ruth 1:6 says that "she had heard in the country of Moab how that the LORD had visited his people in giving them bread." Naomi and her daughters-in-law were at a critical inflection point. Should they continue their relationship? Should they continue to glean strength and strategy from one another and forge on, or should they count their losses and go away with their tails tucked between their legs, back to what they know best?

Initially Orpah and Ruth went with her, but along the way Naomi bid the women to part ways from her. The Scriptures tell us that the women "lifted up their voice, and wept" (Ruth 1:14). Orpah ultimately kissed Naomi good-bye and turned back around to return to her home in Moab, but Ruth decided to follow Naomi back to Judah. In the face of the same grief that crippled Naomi and left her bitter, Ruth makes a brave declaration of faithfulness, both to her mother-in-law and the God of Israel: "Whither thou goest, I will go; and where thou lodgest, I will lodge: thy people shall be my people, and thy God my God" (v. 16).

When faced with the dilemma or decision to continue a relationship, do you consider divine connections, like Ruth did, or has bitterness blinded your vision so that all you see is a worldly obligation to a person, place, entity, or thing, as in the case of Naomi and perhaps Orpah? Who has your bitterness turned you away from? These are questions to consider as we continue this journey toward exposing and removing the root of bitterness and its effects of the silent killer.

When news of Naomi's return to Bethlehem spread, many women came out to greet her. However, when they saw her in her current physical state and heard her complaints about her plight, they wondered, "Could this be Naomi, whose name means 'pleasant'? She looks like a woman who's been in a fight with life and lost! Naomi has been beaten down by life and looks much older and sounds jaded. Is this an impostor? Where's our friend?" the women cried. I imagine they prompted her, "Naomi, speak from what's in your heart, girl!"

So, Naomi turned and told the crowd, "Don't call me Naomi but Mara, because God has dealt bitterly with me! Don't call me pleasant anymore, because I am bitter!" (See Ruth 1:19–21.) The silent killer, better known as bitterness, had claimed her as its victim and taken its toll.

Chapter 2

YOU'VE GOT A RIGHT TO BE MAD

It was not an enemy insulting [scorning;
reproaching] me. I could stand [bear] that. It
was not someone who hated me who insulted
me. I could hide from him. But it is you, a person
like me, my companion and good friend
—PSALM 55:12–13, EXV

THOSE INDIVIDUALS LIVING their lives within the kingdom of God understand there is a war taking place. This war is between the kingdom of light versus the kingdom of darkness. The Bible states, "And from the days of John the Baptist until now the kingdom of heaven suffers violence, and the violent take it by force" (Matt. 11:12, NKJV). Unfortunately, in war there are those who sustain injuries, wounds, and even death by the hand of their own. This is known as friendly fire. Merriam-Webster's dictionary defines *friendly fire* as "the firing of weapons from one's own forces or those of an ally especially when resulting in the accidental death or injury of one's own personnel."[1] According to an article in *The Guardian* by James Meeks, "US troops killed at least seven and wounded 34 of their compatriots in 18 suspected friendly fire incidents after the invasion of Iraq, only the most serious of which have previously been made public, the war logs reveal."[2]

Being injured by a foe is tough; however, it is expected. When two people are engaged in battle or conflict, each person's defenses are heightened, and each is alert to any incoming attacks from their enemy. In a boxing match, before the fight starts, the referee instructs each boxer to protect themselves at all times once the fight starts. With these instructions, the fighters are on high alert, knowing danger is imminent. However, when it comes to being injured by a friend there is no defense strategy or preparation for that surprise attack. To be injured or assaulted by someone you know or called a friend is devastating. It is one of the hardest wounds to heal.

To be injured by someone you trusted or admired can be, and often is, traumatizing. That trauma has a residual affect in the life of the victim. Some see this type of surprise attack as a form of betrayal. That person that was supposed to love them, protect them, counsel them, and even provide for them now has wounded them to their core.

It's like the dog that attacks its own owner; the owner doesn't see it coming. When the dog gnashes out and bites its owner, there is a hideous shrieking sound released that goes thru the heart of its owner. The stare that follows from the owner is of amazement and disbelief. The owner stares at the dog, and in the owner's mind he says, "After all I have done for you and provided for you, this is how you repay me?"

WHISPERINGS OF THE SILENT KILLER

Who wounded you? Do you have the right to be mad?

Many people today are extremely bitter and resentful because of the wounds sustained at the hands of family members, husbands, wives, pastors, and friends, people they knew intimately and trusted. When a person has sustained injuries by the hand of friendly fire it leaves the wounded person in a state of confusion and possibly fear. The bitter person now is forced to consider if there is anyone they can ever truly trust and have confidence in, who can truly have their back without becoming a potential back-stabber.

When a person has been wounded by a friend or loved one they become extremely leery. They look at everyone sideways as if to try and size them up and see what might be hiding behind that kind gesture or bright smile. They become pessimistic and negative. They are often non-trusting and eventually develop a defensive attitude that says, "I will get you before you get me." The wounded person screams out within themselves, saying, "I will never be a victim again!" Now this person's heart is closed, and their emotions are locked away. They walk around numb to life and give up on the chance at true freedom and safety. They ask themselves the question, "Do I have the right to be mad?" There is a quiet whisper from the silent killer telling them, "Yes, you do!" This solidifies their current mind-set, and they proudly become bitter! This reasoning strengthens their position in their heart and mind.

I have sustained many wounds at the hands of my enemies throughout my life. However, there have been none more personal and deeper than those I experienced at the hands of people I loved. I have been involved in romantic relationships in which I believed I was a nice guy, one who gave of his time, efforts, resources, and heart, only to be betrayed in the end. I entered these relationships with hopes and dreams of creating an environment and atmosphere where genuine love, transparency, prosperity, wholeness, and eventually wealth would be the norm; a place where godly principles would be welcomed, celebrated, and embraced, which would yield a life of abundant blessing; a place where God's blessing would be evident to all the outside world. However, it appears in my mind certain people have hidden agendas from the outset. They recognize an easy mark. Their agenda is to take and get as much as they can, and when their bellies and pockets are filled and they think they have found greener pastures elsewhere, they make a sudden exodus—with your goods and heart. The only thing left after these experiences were unanswered questions, shattered dreams, crushed emotions, and a bleeding heart. At that point of bewilderment, I found myself asking myself the question, "Do I have a right to be mad?"

Many people experience similar types of pain in broken marriages, unions that dissolved because of one party's—or both parties'—hidden secrets or destructive proclivities to engage in unhealthy mental or physical activities. When there is ongoing civil war, no genuine unity or love, and a closet full of old unhealed wounds and drawers filled with secrets, success is unrealistic. When this happens, oftentimes people sustain wounds and become bitter and allow the silent killer to come into their lives.

Additionally, you have people who are angry with God because they were born with physical and mental limitations. Sometimes parents bear children with these exceptionalities, and because of this they are extremely bitter with God. These differences, as well as those that result from injuries, can also cause people's own faith to shipwreck. There are those who have chosen to turn their backs on God and remain bitter to this day because of challenges they have experienced since birth or after an injury.

Bitterness can even start in the church. People join churches for various reasons. Some may like the pastor's preaching or the church's vision. Some may like the choir, praise team, the worship style, or the civic outreach programs the church may be involved in. Nonetheless, many people leave these same churches and turn their back on God because of injuries they sustain while at the church. Church hurt is what many people say they have experienced, and because of it they struggle to trust some pastors and the church as an institution. They hold God at fault for allowing the injury to take place. Their rationale is, if God truly loves them, why would He allow them to hurt and hurt within the church? The problem is that too often people trust individuals in places where only God is supposed to occupy. They exalt pastors or other members of the church to a level of praise and expectation that is not appropriate. People are people, and God is God. People fall and fail, but God is perfect and sovereign. He is the only appropriate recipient for our praise. When people hold an improper view of pastors and their church experience, it is inevitable that they will experience hurt while in the church, and the result is that they feel crushed, devastated, and become frigid in their emotions.

I have been a part of ministries where I have witnessed the behind-the-scenes action firsthand. I have seen blatant recklessness and ratchet behavior take place in the name of God. I have witnessed mismanagement of godly resources and the exploitation of God's people, all for selfish gain, control, and notoriety. I have seen pastors whose hearts have become corrupt and greedy for money and who have an entitlement mentality, thus putting their churches and members in compromising positions financially. I have seen some financially affluent members harassed and become targeted because of their financial wealth, as church officers exploit their prosperity while ignoring the real, core issue of the person's life.

Then there are pastors that can see the promise in some of their congregants' life, and instead of developing, training, releasing, and helping to promote that person they discourage them, crushing their dreams—all to retain them in their congregation, which only benefits that pastor.

I have been a part of ministries where other clergy members have tried to sabotage the ministry and cause chaos and division, all for their own selfish gain.

I have witnessed clergy members prey on less fortunate, non-discerning people in order to sexually exploit them in the name of cleansing them or promising them needed resources and promotion within the organization.

Because I was a firsthand witness to these events, the silent killer has attempted multiple times to have me react to heinous events, have a pity party, get angry, and choose to get bitter and hold grudges against these people. I'll admit that in the natural it seemed as if many of these wicked actions had gone unchecked by God. If the truth be told, I almost slipped when I saw the prosperity of the wicked and their actions. I believed I had kept the letter and spirit of the Word, not having yet seen the promises come to fruition. I asked God and myself, "What's wrong with me? Why are my blessings on the slow train to town or continuously delayed?" And I had to ask myself the question, "Do you have the right to be mad about everything?" Of course, the answer is no. The silent killer was working overtime to make me become cynical and pessimistic. It wanted me to become faithless and curse God and myself. It wanted me to stop warring after every prophetic word I ever received about my life to keep them from coming to pass. It wanted me to stop understanding God's plan for me, that life is good.

In the natural I was furious and angry, but I knew that was not the position God would want me to take. I had to learn not to walk in the flesh but the spirit of God. The Spirit of God has allowed me and you the privilege to cast all our cares upon Him because I know He cares for us (1 Pet. 5:7, NKJV). Therefore, we must understand His way of bringing promises and blessings to pass in our life. They may not be at my desired pace, but they are in His timing. So never give up on God!

Remember, these scenarios are very disturbing; however, it is nothing new to mankind—and it is certainly not new to God. King David, when he was just a shepherd boy, was relegated to minimal duty of keeping the sheep. He was rejected by his brothers, not invited to come from the field when the prophet Samuel came to the house. He was an afterthought to his father and brothers, a fact he was confronted with early in his life. But he was the choice of God Himself!

The story of David reads like a motion picture. A boy from the wrong side of the tracks steps into a seemingly impossible situation when he challenges a giant by the name of Goliath to a fight to the death, all to honor God and benefit his family. He is successful in his death match with Goliath, becomes a national hero, brings liberation and respectability to his country once again, marries the king's daughter, and brings prosperity to his family. What a tale!

The truth was, David got the king's daughter but not the king's heart. The Scriptures tell us eventually King Saul began to despise his son-in-law:

> Now it had happened as they were coming home, when David was returning from the slaughter of the Philistine, that the women had come out of all the cities of Israel, singing and dancing, to meet King Saul, with tambourines, with joy, and with musical instruments. So the women sang as they danced, and said: "Saul has slain his thousands, And David his ten thousands." Then Saul was very angry, and the saying displeased him; and he said, "They have ascribed to David ten thousands, and to me they have ascribed only thousands. Now what more can he have but the kingdom?" So Saul eyed David from that day forward.
>
> —1 Samuel 8:6–9, nkjv

If that was not enough to hate him, the prophet prophesied that someday David would be king of Israel in Saul's place!

So, for the next ten or more years, David was on the run because King Saul was trying to kill him. He tried kill him because of his potential and promise, his future blessing to be king.

Now David was displaced from his family, friends, his home, and his wife. He was on the run with misfits and living in caves. He obviously lost his job as the king's harp player. As if this wasn't enough, the king, with all his resources, wanted him dead—all of this because David's heart was in the right place at the right time. Did he have a right to be mad?

When you are confronted with the opportunity to get even, do you take it and release your bitter wrath onto the offending party, or do you take the high road with God? The Scriptures say David was faced with exactly this situation.

> So he came to the sheepfolds by the road, where there was a cave; and Saul went in to attend to his needs. (David and his men were staying in the recesses of the cave.) Then the men of David said to him, "This is the day of which the Lord said to you, 'Behold, I will deliver your enemy into your hand, that you may do to him as it seems good to you.'" And David arose and secretly cut off a corner of Saul's robe. Now it happened afterward

that David's heart troubled him because he had
cut Saul's robe. And he said to his men, "The LORD
forbid that I should do this thing to my master, the
LORD's anointed, to stretch out my hand against
him, seeing he is the anointed of the LORD." So
David restrained his servants with these words,
and did not allow them to rise against Saul.

—1 SAMUEL 26:3–7, NKJV

Here we have a young man with a right to be mad,
someone who had been wounded by friendly fire from
King Saul. He caught the king in a compromising position, a position in which he had the perfect opportunity
to show any bitterness from within his heart and kill
King Saul. But David restrained himself and extended
grace to an undeserving king. Verse 7 says, "The LORD
forbid that I should do this thing to my master, the
LORD's anointed, to stretch out my hand against him,
seeing he is the anointed of the LORD." David had a
right to be mad, but he chose the high road with God's
help. Which would you choose?

If there ever were any person that truly understood what it means to be wounded by friendly fire it
is Jesus. Jesus the all-powerful, Jesus the all-knowing,
the one who hand-picked the apostles, picked two who
would betray Him and hurt Him to his core. Knowing
in advance that the man Judas Iscariot would betray
him, sell him out, and take the blood money had to be
agonizing. For three years, He must have constantly

considered Judas's face and eyes, hoping that somehow, some way, his heart would turn from evil and selfishness and understand he had been chosen to be a part of a world movement that would affect generations to come. But Jesus, when He looked intently into Judas's eyes at the Last Supper, could see that he had already formed a pact with the silent killer of bitterness to carry out the devilish deed. He told the disciples, "The man who has dipped his hand with me into the bowl [probably not a signal, but means 'one who shares close fellowship with me'] is the one who will turn against [betray] me" (Matt. 26:23, EXV).

Often, our anger is tested with people that we have had close fellowship with. Jesus had to tell a prideful Peter what was really in his heart. Jesus said, "I tell you the truth, tonight before the rooster crows you will say three times you don't know me [deny/disown me three times]" (Matt. 26:34, EXV). Can you imagine having the foreknowledge that people you have had close fellowship with, live with, eat with, shared victories with, people you poured your life into, would soon betray you, abandon you, deny you, and, as we already saw, hand you over to murders to kill you? Would you have the right to be mad?

Paul wrote in Ephesians 4:26, "When you are angry [or Be angry, and] do not sin [Ps. 4:4; there is a time for righteous anger, but it must not result in sin], and be sure to stop being angry being the end of the day [don't let the sun set on your anger]" (EXV). There is a time for every activity under heaven, including being angry. Righteous anger is supposed to lead you to Christlike behavior. Acknowledging your true feelings is critical, but reacting in a negative manner that seeks revenge is sinful. Instead, asking God for the courage to respond in a Christlike manner shows meekness and allows you to understand God is yet in control. The Christian must wrap their heart around this truth: "we reap what we sow, more than we sow, and later than we sow."[3] Having the right to become angry is yours, but don't let a right (privilege) become a trap to bring you to a place of bitterness. Remember, the Scriptures say, "So that we may not be outsmarted by Satan. After all, we are not unaware of his intentions" (2 Cor. 2:11, ISV).

Chapter 3

A FAMILIAR STORY

Hope deferred makes the heart sick, but
a dream fulfilled is a tree of life.
—PROVERBS 13:12, NLT

THE IMAGINATION IS one of the most valuable and powerful abilities that human beings possess. The power to dream and imagine incredible events for themselves, their families, and friends is one of the greatest—if not the greatest—gifts. The ability to transport or transcend oneself from his or her current state into a more favorable situation is nothing more than a miracle. Fortunately, this gift is given to everyone; however, it is critical that these dreamers balance their imagination with reality.

Even those who hold this balanced perspective understand life issues can hurt! Life's trials will try to bruise your reality and crush you. Therefore, dreamers must learn to maneuver and maintain their sanity while all along being tried by the vicissitudes of life. Essentially, they must endure while learning to overcome. The person who refuses to be sidetracked or become consumed by hope deferred never finds themselves entertaining, embracing, and harboring bitterness, the stowaway called the silent killer. Those who grasp this revelation or who receive this advice early in their lives from a mentor or encourager are truly blessed. It is a transformative practice.

Unfortunately, I was not the benefactor of someone explaining these truths to me but instead became a victim of life experiences. Like Naomi, I was brought up in a limiting religious environment where there was not enough encouragement. I had an absent father, no mentors, and no spiritual enlightenment. I was just dreaming. Nevertheless, life, as wonderful as it is, and trials, as cruel as they can be, soon taught me you can't live in your imagination only. If so, the results will be disastrous. You will be ill prepared to face the storms and challenges that life brings. Like a trail of devastation left behind after a tornado has passed, the only evidence that there was a life before would be the rubble left behind by the bitter person.

There are those people that say the school of hard knocks is a person's best teacher. For many years, I ascribed to that sentiment; however, once I became a Christian I was challenged. I began to read the Bible for myself. I found there is another option rather than trial and error. The Bible states in Proverbs 9:10 that the "fear of the LORD is the foundation of wisdom. Knowledge of the Holy One results in good judgement"

(NLT). Proverbs also says, "Wisdom is the principal thing; therefore, get wisdom: and with all thy getting get understanding." Lastly, I had to settle within my mind what the Scriptures say in Hebrews 6:18: "By two immutable things, in which was impossible for God to lie..." Truthfully, when I looked at my life, I was troubled about what I found. I had to admit to myself that I was devoid, entirely lacking true, genuine wisdom. I had street smarts, knowledge from trial and error, and knowledge from school but not the wisdom the Bible speaks about. I was suddenly confronted with the choice to believe or not believe what the Bible claims.

Today people have access to great amounts of information about varying topics via the Internet, but this information, this knowledge, often finds its origin in man's opinions or reasoning. There are many strategies and techniques that people can use to handle their issues, and the Internet has made all of these approaches—helpful and not, godly or not—available to everyone. It is imperative to be discerning about what you read, because many such suggestions can become coping mechanisms that just mask the real problem and never get to the root issue of a person's dilemma.

In the world today, as it was in Naomi's times, there were various systems that supposedly offered freedom, power, protection, safety, and wealth. Now, a system may be a belief system, a religion, or clinical institution. Unfortunately, many of these belief systems were and are man-made. What's the problem with man-made systems? First, all are susceptible to human error. They can be filled with flaws, corruption, erosion, mixture, theory, opinions, and demonic influences with limiting, counterfeit power. Additionally, a person's affiliation with and acceptance in these systems will be based on their performance and actions. They won't know the truth of this until they've spent some time interacting with them.

Systems like these offer no authentic dialogue with God. There is no spiritual deliverance taking place, no altering of the way one thinks or live and what one's values are. Nor are there any life-changing miracles, no wonders to be revealed, and most assuredly, no inner healings or breakthroughs. These types of systems are impotent and are not equipped to assist anyone in eradicating a spirit of bitterness out of their lives. These systems are incapable of any real impartation of *agape* love and wisdom. Its subscribers are powerless to become eternal and spiritually minded and become more forgiving of those who offended them. They are ignorant of the need to begin with forgiving themselves and the need to always begin with believing and trusting in God even in the face of pain, peril, and unsurmountable odds. With an adopted mind-set that interprets that all events in their lives will turn out for their development and good, they realign their focus. They will no longer see their problems only, but will see them in the light of a divine Problem Solver who has all the answers. As they continue only to believe and live a life of faith and not doubt, bitterness will be averted from their lives.

But let me clarify: Belief in God is just the beginning. If you recall from James 2:19, even the devils believe there is one God. Believing in God's existence, His power, and His teachings is one thing. However, choosing to consistently embrace and incorporate those teachings into your life is another. I have had to learn there are benefits to having a fresh, thriving relationship with God and remaining obedient to His teachings. It yields a life of continuous blessings, breakthrough, and power in my life and to anyone that would embrace this philosophy. There are many people who believe in that God exists, but they lack commitment. They do not have a defined regimen in place that yields a constant audience with God. Many Christians choose to seek the provisions, promises, and blessings only and refuse to create intimacy with God. They forfeit the most important aspect of having a relationship with Him. To be honest, I have found myself performing the letter of the law (keeping the rules) but at other times and seasons neglecting the spirit of the law. God said, "Obedience is better than sacrifice" (1 Sam. 15:22, NLT).

Once we learn this truth, what would keep a person from cultivating the most treasured, most life-changing relationship available? Fear, pride and laziness. Fear says, "I would not be accepted." Pride says, "I don't really need that relationship. I refuse to be codependent on an entity for provision, blessings, directions, or safety."

Last, laziness says, "It would take too much work. I can take or leave it! I would have to give up too much of my life for it to work. Besides, I believe in God already! I will leave that relationship for the deep folks." Fear and pride are tormenting, damaging spirits that come to sabotage a person's progress in life. These spirits can provoke a person to make foolish decisions.

Pride is a false estimation of one's self. This spirit mainly enters as the result of ignorantly believing every achievement, ability, and gift is self-given. Also, pride gains power when people begin to perceive the applauses of men to be their endorsement and validation. It also commonly afflicts individuals through bloodline curses.

A swarming effect comes over a person's mind when fear takes over. They become consumed with information about their situation. I have been overwhelmed with situations or circumstances in certain periods of my life. I have been overwhelmed because of a series of life failures, setbacks, and unexplained events; overwhelmed because of hope deferred, traumatic events, and simply one let down after another. I succumbed and became jaded and gave in to the silent killer's spell and lived in a self-imposed spiritual and mental state of bitterness.

The spirits of pride, fear, and laziness can penetrate a person's spirit in several ways. The first way is through ignorance. What you don't know can literally kill you! Second, they can gain entry through a traumatic event in a person's life in which proper healing has not taken place. Third, fear, pride, and laziness can gain a foothold through transgenerational bloodline curses.

Bitterness and the Cycle of Pain

When people take a survey of their life, if a pattern of perceived devastation and failure is detected, some may try to find a connection between their socioeconomic status, health, or relationships and their failures, such as the inability to maintain gainful employment; failure at advancing in their career, at their own business, or at ministry; failure at establishing rewarding relationships, at love, losing weight, being a role model for their children, or at being present in the moment with their children or spouse. If the individual believes they had limited amounts of opportunities to succeed, they often find themselves yielding to external voices or vices to cope with life. They self-medicate, turning to questionable behavior and in the process subconsciously becoming cynical and hard-hearted. Some may choose to overeat, some turn to alcohol and drugs, some constantly party and become very promiscuous, and others turn to a life of crime. These are all external vices that serve nothing more than to complicate their situation and mask the real problem. After self-medicating with these habits, they still find themselves with no lasting relief from the pain of the event, leaving them more wounded and creating the perfect environment for bitterness to take root.

Other people cope with pain by trying to escape

mentally until they feel stronger and can face their problems. Elimelech and Naomi chose to physically escape their circumstances for this same reason. They sojourned to the country of Moab because there was a famine in the land and they were seeking safety, provision, and assurance. In the past I have found myself traveling to what I deem a far country, also seeking safety and provision. While there, I came to the stunning revelation that you can't run away from yourself and issues. Like Elimelech who began to assimilate into the society and embrace the culture, I ran from my failures and found myself accepting a lifestyle that was less than God's call for my life. I learned that this temporary journey only ever turns out to be another problem just being compounded on existing problems. Pain and problems seem to lead to bitterness, which leads to further pain and further problems.

Given this cycle of hurt, it seems there may be truth in the old phrase, "Misery loves company." In some instances, like mine, people's pain and frustration sometimes go unnoticed, further solidifying their bitterness. In so many other cases, though, pain is extremely visible and vocal. There are people watching and making mental notes about your pain, setbacks, and your reactions to them. Perhaps that's why we see people's issues plastered all over the airwaves and across magazine covers. In our voyeuristic culture, pain sells. Everything around us screams, "Bitterness stories on sale today! Get it while it's hot. Only $5.99!" People love to watch others' lives encounter a train wreck, and billions of dollars have been made and lost in the pursuit of this sort of fame. We too often look at people like an episode of *Lifestyles of the Rich and Famous*. However, unlike reality TV, where there is a TV camera always recording every move you make, capturing how you respond to life, pain, and offense, the origin of many people's bitterness, like mine, went unrecorded, and all I was left with was a bitter manifested self—and no one wants to watch that play out. That's the thing about bitterness; it always shows somehow. It is not as easy to conceal as pain. It wants to be expressed.

Naomi did not have an opportunity to conceal her pain and grief when she lost her husband, nor her bitterness when her sons died suddenly. Nevertheless, like reality TV, the viewers were watching. The world saw everything. Orpah and Ruth were watching how Naomi filtered life's toughest moments and taking mental notes. My family and friends have also done this, being present and witnessing how I handled my issues. However, there were no cameras following me. There are no cameras following you around today. But when unpleasant events occurred or someone offended you or betrayed you, how did you respond? Did your bitterness show through like grey hairs fighting their way through a patch of dark hair?

When Naomi's sons died and she decided to return to her home in Bethlehem, she had the opportunity to be a mentor and comforter to her daughters-in-law. After all, they too had suffered a devastating loss. Maturity rises its head at appropriate times and should be a comfort and healing balm to others that may be hurting. On the other hand, bitterness is reckless. It is oblivious to anyone else's pain but its own. So, we have Naomi telling the young ladies to separate from her and return to their mothers' homes. We find in Ruth 1:8–13 that Naomi was trying to spare the girls from any further pain and disappointment. Either way, it revealed a lack of sensitivity on Naomi's part, and that's how bitter people can be portrayed.

The bitter person is likened to a crude, heartless coach who tells you to suck it up, stop your whining, and move on! Their approach is more like abrasive sandpaper than like a soft pillow you rest your head on. Instead of being an atmosphere refresher, they pollute the atmosphere and everyone in it with their cynical, self-absorbed attitude. Naomi's attitude caused one of her daughters-in-law to turn away hurt, depressed, and sad. Even in our toughest moments of life, we have the responsibility not to injure or bring hopelessness to our fellow man, regardless of what we maybe currently enduring. We never know who else is on the verge of giving in to the silent killer of bitterness.

To justify having a root of bitterness in the heart, a bitter person will often chronicle the events surrounding their bad luck. They will keep the facts fresh in their mind; they rehearse the names, places, dates, and events that surrounded the negativity. It runs on a continuous loop in their mind. If this person never receives any genuine deliverance they are sentenced to a life of torment and pain. If anyone asks or if something or someone triggers a negative thought in the bitter person's mind, the negativity comes spewing out like a volcanic eruption, like lava oozing out and contaminating and wounding everything in its path.

As we discussed before, upon Naomi's return to Bethlehem, women met her upon her arrival. Who knows, maybe it was friends, neighbors, and people who cared about her in the crowd; maybe it was naysayers. Regardless, before they could embrace and celebrate her return properly, they were introduced to the spirt of bitterness. This spirit was grumpy, harsh, sharp, rude, and had a bad disposition.

> When they came to Bethlehem, the entire town was excited by their arrival. "Is it really Naomi?" the women asked. "Don't call me Naomi," she responded. "Instead, call me Mara, for the Almighty has made life very bitter for me. I went away full, but the LORD has brought me home empty. Why call me Naomi when the LORD has caused me to suffer and the Almighty has sent such tragedy upon me?
> —RUTH 1:19–21, NLT

Naomi was instructed, under this spirit's direction, to explain why she did not want to be called by her old name. Naomi means "pleasant." Her new name of Mara, which was more fitting for who she was in her current state and station in life, means "bitter." Her bitterness became her identity. She had begun to blame God for her plight. From her vantage point, He was the author of her pain, and there was nothing she could have done to prevent the disaster.

I was like Naomi! I blamed everyone, including God, for my pain, for what I did not have, and the unfair treatment I had endured. One day I came to this realization: I may not have deserved what happened to me, nor did I have any control over what happened to me; however, I did have the ability to control how I felt about myself. I did not have to create a new persona to tell people, "Yes, indeed, I am bitter." I realized that I controlled how I allowed events to affect my life. I had to stop nursing the wounds of my past, stop negative memory recall, stop blaming others, and choose to forgive all my offenders. Only then could I began to live life in a forward direction again.

Are you living life in a forward direction? If not, why? I want you to take a few minutes to look inward prayerfully and ask the Holy Spirit to reveal any manifestations of this spirit of bitterness in your life and behavior. It may be helpful to reflect first on negative experiences or trauma in your past. Feel free to turn back to the list of negative experiences in the introduction and the different sources of offense in the previous chapter. In the aftermath of these situations, how did you respond? Did you turn to the Lord, your fortress in times of trouble, the one who calls you a victor in every season? Or did it break you down, causing you to perceive yourself differently and as a victim? If the latter, you may be harboring the silent killer.

As you continue to read this book, I encourage you to remain prayerful and open to receiving revelation from the Lord about the state of your heart. If you are in an accountability relationship with another trusted and faithful believer, it may be wise to ask them to pray with you and help keep you accountable for staying on the path of total healing and wholeness.

Sometimes when people begin to open up their heart to total healing the Holy Spirit allows repressed memories of trauma to come to mind. This is often painful—sometimes very much so—but it is necessary in order to receive deliverance. If you find that this happens to you as you search your heart for bitterness and its source, do not allow the memory of that pain to cause you to stumble or stall out in your journey. Let it make you more determined than ever to move forward and tenaciously seek the freedom that is yours in Christ. Today is the day to claim your freedom from the silent killer!

Chapter 4

A CONVERSATION ABOUT
BITTERNESS

Be careful [See to it; Take heed] that no one
fails to receive [falls short of] God's grace and
begins to cause trouble among you [that no
bitter root/plant grows up to cause trouble].
—HEBREWS 12:15, EXV

NAOMI GREW UP hearing the rabbi recite the Scriptures at synagogue. She was raised in an environment in which she heard about the ways of God and saw the favor of God in her family's life. She understood God is a caring God that understands all our fights and situations. So, why did she not just admit she needed help with her anger, which morphed into bitterness? The answer is this: Who did Naomi have left that she could confide in about her bitterness? Who did she have left that could have empathized with her? What friend or spiritual leader could she talk to about her true feelings and at the same time learn about the destructive nature of bitterness?

Proverbs 27:17 states, "As iron sharpens iron, so a friend sharpens a friend" (NLT), but Naomi lacked the sort of friendship that holds this transformative power.

Why was Naomi unable to see God had a history of restoring and renewing what once was dead? Why was she unable to see, regardless of the facts of her life, that with God she still could be victorious in this tough situation? Living in Moab away from other believers caused Naomi to suffer spiritually. Living in a pagan society that did not have the same beliefs really added to the erosion of Naomi's spiritual life. Hebrews 10:25 compels believers not to forsake "the assembling of ourselves together." Naomi missed out on the synergy of being around other like believers. As a result, her level of trust in God was not where it should have been. Romans 8:28 states, "We know that in everything God works [or God works everything together...] for the good of those who love him. They are the people he called, because that was his plan [...according to his purpose]" (EXV). God understands that man often looks for another way or options to solving problems. However, He pleads with man and tells man to allow Him to be his first and only option to resolve conflict and hurt in his life. Naomi surely grappled with this as she returned to Bethlehem and the accountability of her people.

Unfortunately, like so many believers, it seems she grappled with this alone. There is no evidence in the Scriptures that any of the women who greeted her as she and Ruth entered Bethlehem approached her about her declaration that she was no longer Naomi but Mara. There is no evidence that she even discussed it with Ruth. How could this be?

All over the world, on any given day and time, there are innumerable conversations taking place. These conversations take place at different levels of society. They take place on a global level, which could surround topics such as oil prices, terrorist attacks, or G8 summit updates. On a national level, the conversations often revolve around topics or events taking place within that country. Here in the United States they are many conversations taking place on the topic of President Donald Trump. These specific conversations regarding President Trump often deal with the approval or disapproval of him as president and him as a person. Additional discussions could range from topics such as immigration and travel ban restrictions to rights for the LGTB community, issues of economic inequality, and race.

Likewise, there are conversations taking place within specific regions. Here in Chicago, there are several main topics constantly being discussed, such as the murder rate in 2016–2017, the low number of law enforcement officers, lack of funding for the public schools across the Chicago footprint, the high level of unemployment, and rising of property taxes.

When it comes to conversations of a personal nature, people discuss topics such as lack of money, utility bills, children's safety, romantic relationships or the lack thereof, the latest trends, family members, social media, and what's taking place at church. However, it is very rare that people spend much time having real dialogue about the bitterness in their lives, though it is an emotional and spiritual condition that affects millions worldwide. Unfortunately, bitterness has such a negative connotation attached to it that people avoid having conversations about the topic.

It appears that people don't want to be labeled as a bitter person or connected with someone who maybe bitter. As a result, this topic is not discussed adequately. Many people just dismiss it or overlook it all together. However, if a person is bitter and they refuse to confront the issue, it could have devastating consequences in their life because of neglect or refusing to confront the elephant in their lives. Evangelist Paula White suggests you must confront negative issues.[1] She further states, "You cannot conquer what you will not confront." Dr. George Simon concurs and goes on to describe what bitterness does. In his article titled "Confronting the High Cost of Bitterness" he states, "Bitterness settles in when someone encapsulates and 'freezes' in place anger over emotional injuries that were suffered in the past."[2]

To get an accurate description of what bitterness is and how it negatively affects people, there must first be an accepted description and definition of what it is exactly. Webster's Dictionary describes *bitterness* as "distasteful or distressing to the mind...caused by or expressive of severe pain, grief, or regret."[3] S. I. McMillian, author of the book *None of These Diseases*, states, "Anger unhandled will show itself in at least 50 diseases";[4] bitterness is a form of anger, so the same may be said of it. Dr. Norm Wright, a psychology professor at Biola University, agrees with McMillian. He writes that bitterness disturbs the alimentary canal, which runs from the throat to the rectum. This disturbance produces colitis, diarrhea, ulcers, and mental illness.[5] Spiritually, bitterness brings the individual to a "stuck state," a place where you are unable to access and acknowledge your situation properly. You become unable to accept God's love of forgiveness, causing doubts about God to settle in your heart. From these descriptions we can conclude bitterness is not a healthy emotional or spiritual state to be in. We see this from the negative physical, mental, and spiritual affect that bitterness can have on the human body.

The first thing we must understand is bitterness does not discriminate, nor is it a mental disorder for the mentally challenged individual. It is an equal-opportunity imprisoner! This condition affects the affluent. It affects the politically established and the downtrodden. It affects people in every sphere and segment of society; therefore, there is no segment of society where bitterness can't be found. What is obvious is that there are many people worldwide who live in a state of bitterness and have its root lodged deep within their heart.

One of the biggest misconceptions of life is that bitterness is a normal progression of the human experience, that when a person arrives at a certain age he or she automatically just transitions into becoming a bitter man or woman. This is a giant misconception that some believe. This is a lie! Jesus stated in John 10:10 that He came that we may have life and "have it more abundantly." When a person allows themselves to become bitter, they must understand they are making a conscious decision to choose to be offended. They are making a decision not to forgive the offender, no matter who the offender may be. This choice is because the offense they feel they have sustained was so egregious that it seems impossible for them to forgive and move on.

If bitterness entrenches itself and grows unchecked out of a person's heart, that person will surely live a life of mental torment. A bitter person will exhibit manifestations of unexplained frustrations, display resentment, and will adopt an unforgiving spirit, and that torment will have a negative effect on their body.

To determine if a person is harboring bitterness, you must be able to discern certain characteristics. Below is a list of characteristics a bitter person may display:

1. Feeling jaded

2. Holding grudges

3. Being jealous

4. Drawing comparison

5. Seeking attention

6. Being negative

Individuals that display these characteristics may be harboring bitterness. A person that displays feelings of being jaded are prone to believe that some person or persons have singled them out in some manner that segregates them. This is a person that holds grudges and believes they have a valid reason to do so and are justified in continuing to harbor resentment and bitterness. Feelings of jealousy or comparison come from the belief that other people's strengths highlight their weakness. An attention-seeking person wants assurance they are right in their stance and are just as good as anyone else. A person who displays feelings of negativity is a person who has issues with themselves but refuses to or is unable to celebrate anything or anyone being positive.

There are many reasons the Bible exhorts believers to stay in fellowship with one another, but one of the greatest benefits is the role trusted, faithful friends can have in our spiritual growth and development. It is a challenge to identify the symptoms of bitterness in ourselves. Too often we tend to have blind spots when it comes to shortcomings that are rooted in our pain or trauma. We must rely on accountability partners in our Christian community to help us identify and acknowledge these areas. Then, once you have decided to acknowledge that you are indeed bitter and are harboring this spirit, you must also be willing to entertain conversations about eradicating the bitter root. If you are serious about seeking wholeness in your heart, you must continue to take the appropriate steps, which we will discuss in later chapters, and then consult with a trusted Christian leader. This fellowship is essential for getting and staying free.

Chapter 5

IT'S TIME TO DEAL WITH
THE SILENT KILLER

They are blessed who work for peace
[blessed are the peacemakers], for they will
be called God's children [or sons].
—MATTHEW 5:9, EXV

ONFLICT RESOLUTION IS not at the top of many people's priority list. Rather than deal with a problem head on, people often find it more convenient and, frankly, easier to avoid the offending party. Understand this approach is not a long-term fix at all! If a bad tooth is left unaddressed or avoided in the decaying process, that tooth will cause extreme discomfort and pain. Bitterness is like that annoying and decaying tooth, its pain lasting perhaps for days, weeks, or months. That bitterness is surely going to cause trouble, like the throbbing pain of a decaying tooth. Avoidance, with no intention to resolve the conflict or forgive the offender, does nothing more than delay any possible restoration. Avoidance of any kind often does not help at all.

It's important to understand that anyone with bitterness should face their true feelings and talk about their current emotional state of bitterness and anger. Unfortunately, this included Naomi. As we view the life of Naomi, we see that bitterness had been building up for quite a while. This was a result of all the unfortunate events that had taken place in her life and her family's decisions. She needed to understand remaining bitter is not a good idea. It would leave her in a stuck place in her emotions, stalled on the emotional highway of life. Every day she continued to harbor bitterness she increased the risk of becoming a pessimistic person with a grim outlook on life and about God. The bitterness, in the long haul, could affect her health and mental stability as well. Therefore, it behooved her to bring her feelings to a resolution. She had to choose to address this issue head on and engage with the silent killer, using biblical strategies to eliminate him from her life for good.

You may be facing the same decision today. Are you willing and ready to deal with the silent killer?

WE'VE GOT TO GROW UP

Within many cultures and here in the United States, some believe forgiving a person is a sign of weakness. Many think that if they are labeled soft or a pushover they open themselves up to future assaults or ill treatment from random abusers. As a result, unforgiveness becomes a wall of protection. It is a wall that can't be penetrated from the outside.

Bitterness is something they learn to live with, much like an ugly wart. They know they want it removed, but they do nothing about it. They seem to co-exist together, but because bitterness is a thief and a robber it slowly robs them from lasting peace. Bitterness repositions the bitter person so that forgiveness is not welcome because they are paralyzed in their soul. Bitterness brings physical, emotional, and spiritual harm to the person harboring it. Bitterness is destructive in nature. There is no solace in taking and maintaining anger. Listen, people should want to be at peace with one another and with themselves!

A person living with a spirit of bitterness will exhibit signs of arrested development. This is a condition many people find themselves in because of some offense or assault they sustained. They were unable or unwilling to face the reality of the offense to find a strategy or method for receiving healing. Anneli Rufus wrote an article for *Psychology Today* in which she describes the result of this phenomena:

> Some of us look grown-up but aren't. We walk around with suits and briefcases and car keys and annuities. But inside, we are five. Ten. Twelve. Sixteen. We sit in boardrooms, travel the world, even write books. But we are kids, still playing

> dress-up, playing house. *Our bodies matured but
> our minds did not.* Now—playing catch-up, playing
> spy—we feel left out of the adult world, certain
> that our would-be peers are whimpering behind
> our backs, or speaking in code we do not know.
> See? What a childish fear, right there. They're all
> talking in code.[1] (emphasis added)

Arrested development is not just a new term for the twenty-first century. It is an ancient demonic spirit with an agenda that's been derailing men and women for centuries. This spirit causes the person to forfeit God's best for their lives because they are stuck in their soul. Arrested development does not just attack the downtrodden. It affects people in every segment of society. It is unnatural for people to stop maturing physically, emotionally, intellectually, or spiritually. Growth in life is expected, and there is a proper process to growth.

A healthy, natural growth process of humans should be birth, infancy, adolescence, adulthood, and finally, becoming a senior citizen. Then there is a spiritual growth pattern as well. It is important to know that human beings do indeed possess a spiritual component to their makeup. Man has a body, a mind, and a spirit! According to 3 John 1–2, humans can be whole and healthy in their mind, body, and soul. This scripture describes the areas where we need total soundness. This scripture allows the believer to understand there is a proper spiritual growth process, and anyone who believes in the teachings of the Bible should grow therein.

The pattern of spiritual growth follows this progression:

1. Coming into faith

2. Growing in faith

3. Milk to solid food

4. Student to teacher

5. Exhibit maturity

6. Worldly priorities to spiritual priorities

7. Distinguish false doctrine from truth

8. Show stability

When the natural or spiritual patterns of growth are suddenly halted as a result of some type of trauma, that person's growth is often arrested. It stops. If the person does not receive some type of outside intervention, some healing or restoration, the person runs the risk of becoming deformed and dysfunctional in their growth cycle. People who suffer from arrested development often grow into bitter people. These people usually have been injured or wounded in their emotions and soul. Many were the victims of various types of abuse and abandonment. They suffer from identity issues. They may live in an extreme situation, like poverty. One thing they all have in common is they are all stuck and have grown bitter.

The only solution is to grow up. There is nothing pleasant, nor beneficial, about becoming bitter or harboring bitterness. So why don't more people who are bitter confront their condition? Pain and more pain! Many simply refuse to relive the emotional pain of the offense at all costs. The people taking this position must understand that distance from offense is not the same as being delivered and healed from the offense. As I mentioned before, time does not heal all wounds. Deliverance does not come automatically the more you push off the thought of the hurts and offenses you've experienced. Deliverance is a deliberate act! It's posturing oneself in an environment so that confrontation is possible. Acknowledging, identifying, and diagnosing the hurt and pain of the offense is inevitable and expected in this type of setting. It is this courageous act that sets the stage for a bitter person to confront the elephant in their heart, mind, and soul and finally move on to the next level of spiritual and emotional maturity.

Your Health Is Not Just About You

We are living in a time of lawlessness. It is a time and season where, after being offended, men and women are taking matters into their own hands. They often don't stop and think about the negative consequences that their anger and unaddressed bitterness will cause them and their loved ones. The Bible states in Proverbs

25:28, "Like a city that is broken down and without walls [leaving it unprotected] Is a man who has no self-control over his spirit [and sets himself up for trouble]" (AMP).

If you are struggling with bitterness, it is important to confront the spirit of bitterness not just for yourself but also for the next generation of people around you. Like reality TV cameras that always seem to be capturing all the drama of the reality stars as they implode, children that live with bitter people are mentally capturing and absorbing all the mental and verbal outbursts from the bitter person. They witness all the mood swings and wonder, Why is Mama or Daddy always angry? The child of a bitter person may wonder why certain types of conversations, people, TV shows, and songs seem to trigger a negative response in their family member's memory. If the child is not taught that negative outbursts are not normal, the child can adopt the mind-set that this behavior is acceptable and that this is how you deal with people who may have offended them in some fashion.

It is important to pass on to our children that there is a proper way to handle conflict and offense. There is a proper way to handle a conflict to yield a favorable outcome that ends in forgiveness. Forgiveness is a powerful gift. It is an ability that every human being possesses. We can release an offender, no matter how egregious or horrendous the offense was. Parents should always pass on positive character traits, like forgiveness, to their children. It helps to enrich and educate their children's lives. Positive character traits help to position the child for success.

Children almost always repeat what they see their parents, mentors, or leaders do over what they tell them not to do. Therefore, if the offended party chooses not to forgive but attempt revenge, they are teaching their children to be revengeful and to take matters into their own hands. They are teaching their children that it is acceptable to return evil for evil, leaving no thought or room for restoration and renewal. It even leaves the door open to the possibility of violence.

A NATIONAL EPIDEMIC

The Constitution of the United States is a wonderful document. There are elements of the Constitution that allow people to voice their opinions on varying subjects. However, the expression of opinions or freedom of speech can and often is used as a fiery arrow of offense when it is not filtered properly. Once the arrow hits the target it causes an explosion. When healing has not been allowed to progress at the appropriate pace, even an attempt at genuine restitution does nothing more than help foster the spirit of bitterness, fanning the flames.

A perfect example of this is the current state of race relations in the United States today. Modern-day African American grapple with generations of trauma, which stems from centuries of inequitable treatment and outright persecution. Attempts have been made at restitution for the years during which slavery was permitted and endorsed, but for many, the wound has never been allowed to heal because of constant reminders of the past and continued discrimination. When people use their freedom of expression to display memorabilia from the past that stood for this inequality and hate, that promoted violence or helped to foster hate—memorabilia as simple as the Confederate flag—that person's exercise of their liberty does nothing more than rip open wounds that were thought to have healed. It becomes a stumbling block to healing, making even those attempts that have been made at restitution fall short.

This type of bitterness runs deep within the United States. Jewish Americans, Native Americans, African-Americans, and other ethnic groups still have to live with the pain of what happened to their ancestors. Even though laws may have been passed to ensure more equality for them, the sting of the memory of their persecution remains. Laws only mask or cover up the offense as if it never happened. A subliminal message is sent to the abused population to just get over it and move on. This type of insensitivity enrages people and provokes them to become very bitter. This bitterness builds up like steam in a pressure cooker until the person cannot help but release the tension. Sometimes, like a pressure release valve, it comes out in an outburst of outspoken frustration. Sometimes—when even the pressure release valve has been closed off and shut up for too long—it comes out as an explosion. In these scenarios, people's pain and bitterness becomes visual and can be seen through demonstrations, marches, sit-ins, and sometimes even violence.

On the other hand, there are many people who live with bitterness and don't try to conceal it, nor do they deny that they are bitter. In their case, the pressure never builds; it is constantly being released in an endless stream of outbursts. These people feel that they are justified in their position as it relates to harboring bitterness. *Justification* is a legal word that is often used in courts of law, though many people invoke this legal term to make excuses for their position and reasoning in continuing to remain bitter. In the Bible, *justification* is a term used to describe a believer's position with God, especially after they have confessed their sins, asked for forgiveness, and returned to God. In this process, the God of the Bible releases them of their sin, and the believer is restored back to Him. There is no longer any enmity between man and God at that point.

When the bitter person takes the position of justifying their bitterness, they are really saying, "I refuse to be reconciled with that person or people." Their mindset demonstrates a belief that the offender is beyond redemption and there is absolutely no chance to be reconciled to their offender. This continues the demonic cycle of bitterness and allows it to spread and grow roots.

These roots eventually entangle themselves around the heart of the offended. At this point, the offended is stuck and is not attempting to get relief or release from their pain.

The only cure for the epidemic of bitterness in our nation is for individuals across the United States to recognize and accept that yesterday is the past, today is the present, and tomorrow will reveal people's destiny. Any person that chooses to harbor bitterness and not offer forgiveness—the olive branch of divine love—is tampering with their divine destiny and allowing the silent killer to claim them as a victim.

Man's attempt at healing offenses and emotional wounds—with his medications, support groups, and ten-step programs—may seem decisive and time-tested, but the God of the Bible left life-saving solutions for unforgiveness in the Scriptures millennia ago. Matthew 18:21 tells us this about forgiveness: "Then Peter came to him and asked, 'Lord, how many times will my brother sin against me and I forgive him and let it go? Up to seven times?' Jesus answered him, 'I say to you, not up to seven times, but seventy times seven" (AMP). This scripture is not saying to forgive only forty-nine times but to have a mind-set of continuous forgiveness. This type of mind-set does not create a soft person or a pushover but a person that will seek God's help—and we need God's strategy to live a life free of bitterness. We must leave the revenge up to God. You reap what you sow, and it's time to sow forgiveness so that we can reap healing.

Chapter 6

APPREHENDING THE SILENT KILLER

And I will give you the keys of the kingdom
of heaven, and whatever you bind on earth
will be bound in heaven and whatever you
loose on earth will be loosed in heaven.
—MATTHEW 16:19, NKJV

E ARE LIVING in perilous times, a time when evil is on the loose all over the earth. Manifestations of evil can be seen in people's lives. Because of this reality, we must deal with evil and its manifestations head on. They can no longer be given immunity. Evil cannot continue to wreak havoc in our lives. We must apprehend it. The silent killer, this spirit of bitterness, must be apprehended and put under arrest in the life of the believer. Looking at natural strategies can point us in the right direction.

The United States of America has an internal agency, the Federal Bureau of Investigation, that exists to protect its citizens. The FBI has two criteria that it examines when considering if someone qualifies for the FBI's

Ten Most Wanted list. This is an infamous list of people who have terrorized and committed heinous crimes against humanity. First, they ask questions such as, "Is this person a danger to society? Is this person violent? Armed? Does he or she have a long history of serious criminal behavior?"[1] Second, they ask, "Would the publicity offered by a position on Ten Most Wanted list provide a much better chance of catching this person? If the person is already famous by other means, he or she would probably not be chosen for the list because it would be a waste of publicity. The list is intended to provide tremendous publicity to aid in catching a fugitive who might otherwise remain obscure and unrecognizable."[2] Highlighting attention on a certain subject does several things. Primarily, it brings awareness to what crime was committed and identifies the assailant, therefore publicizing their identity and indiscretion so the public at large can assist with the search and eventual capture.

As it is in the natural, so it is in the spirit. The spirit of bitterness is a constant threat and has been terrorizing people for centuries. It is operating under a position of spiritual immunity. No longer can this demon be allowed to continue his assault on mankind. He must be stopped and apprehended, incarcerated in the pit of hell.

In the natural, an arrest warrant is issued by the Department of Justice, the legal arm of the government, empowering the FBI with power to arrest and apprehend the wanted individual. Biblically, Jesus empowers and deputizes His obedient followers with the power to arrest. He instructed and informed believers by saying, "And I will give you the keys of the kingdom of heaven, and whatever you bind on earth will be bound in heaven, and whatever you loose on earth will be loosed in heaven" (Matt. 16:19, NKJV). To bring the believer to a place of confidence, Jesus assured His followers of His authority and power. He stated, "I assure you and most solemnly say to you, whatever you bind [forbid, declare to be improper and unlawful] on earth shall have [already] been bound in heaven, and whatever you loose [permit, declare lawful] on earth shall have [already] been loosed in heaven" (Matt. 18:18, AMP).

In the natural, law enforcement has a constitutional right and obligation to maintain order in society and remove, apprehend, and possibly imprison law breakers. In the spirit, Christians have the biblical right, authority, and obligation to apprehend, bind, and expel all agents of hell, including the spirit of bitterness. The problem is in the doing. There must be a sense of urgency in the heart of people that have been hurt, plagued, and wounded before apprehension will ever take place. One thing is certain: the authority to apprehend is there, but the will or desire to eliminate and eradicate the silent killer is a matter of definite choice. We should have enough empowered believers who have a burden to apprehend the silent killer, but sadly, the body of Christ is lacking Christians who will go after this member of heaven's most wanted. Jesus told His followers the disciples, "There are many people to harvest [The harvest is great/large] but there are only a few workers [the workers/ laborers are few]." We can see the parallel between the natural and spiritual realms.

When the natural and spiritual authorities do not stand up to be held accountable and responsible, then lawlessness and anarchy will prevail. The Bible states Jesus is the origin of all power. Jesus stated, "All power in Heaven and over earth has been given to me" (Matt. 28:18, WNT). If that is true, then why do many people ignore this truth? Why do so many continue to confront bitterness with man-made remedies and strategies? Some have even tried to eradicate bitterness with medicine or psychological theory. Could it be that many find it easier to trust in self instead of the finished work of Jesus Christ? Why do so many people still refuse to trust the power of Jesus, the risen Savior and King of kings? It is time for believers to use their God-given authority to destroy the work of the spirit of bitterness.

TAKING DOWN ONE OF HEAVEN'S MOST WANTED

Human beings are endowed with the ability to display many emotions in life, but some people choose to ignore their feelings. This isn't to say that they don't have them or that they are turning them over to the Lord; pretending you aren't experiencing an emotional reaction when you are can be even more dangerous than placing too much emphasis on emotions. When emotions are dealt with improperly, the flesh is put on a pedestal, taking away control of the spirit and creating an open door for the spirit of bitterness to set up camp.

Many people ignorantly choose to fight this ancient spirit with chemical dependencies and some with venting their frustration to other people. They walk around with a short fuse, often becoming what they despise most, an offender. These human strategies are fruitless against this spiritual foe. Just as the FBI has the authority to create joint task forces with other agencies to help in the apprehension of a criminal, joint effort is required in taking down the spirit of bitterness. The offended party must solicit God's help in the matter. He alone is qualified to help equip the believer with strength and strategy.

God is an all-knowing God; therefore, He is very aware without His intervention it is utterly impossible for some to forgive because of the nature of the offense. He says in Romans 5:8, "But God shows [demonstrates; proves] his great [own] love for us in this way: Christ died for us while we were still sinners" (EXV). God is saying when the Christian was at his worst, before he knew God or had a personal relationship with God, he was an enemy of God's. But God saw his innumerable flaws and decided to forgive him. He decided to die, save, and pardon his sin. So, He expects the Christian to follow His example and choose to forgive. A person is only able to take this posture if they believe in the teachings of the Bible and handle life's tough situations the way that God instructs them to. That's why it is impossible to become completely delivered from the silent killer if you are not living a life surrendered to the Lord.

As I said before, believing in God is not enough. To identify, apprehend, and incarcerate the spirit of bitterness, you must be walking in relationship with the Lord every day. This means acknowledging that you are not your own. The Holy Scriptures tell us:

> Or do you not know that your body is the temple of the Holy Spirit who is in you, whom you have from God, and you are not your own? For you were bought at a price; therefore glorify God in your body and in your spirit, which are God's.
> —1 CORINTHIANS 6:19–20, NKJV

Metaphorically, Jesus went into the slave auction of life and purchased man's freedom from the devil. He paid Satan, the slave owner, with His own blood to redeem our life. As His purchased property, we have a debt to live the way He dictates. This means including Him on all our important life decisions to bring him glory and honor and to show God we trust Him and appreciate His love for us and our life. Can you say this is true of your life? If so, that's wonderful! You're ready to embark on the steps below to gaining freedom—to gaining your life back! If not, it's time to make a decision. Are you ready to surrender your life, your emotions, and your will to the Lord completely? Yes? Then say the prayer below with me:

> *Dear Lord, I humbly and respectfully come into Your presence today. I first would like to acknowledge that I need You as the driving force of my life. Second, I want to acknowledge that, yes, I have been harboring the spirit of bitterness in my heart. I finally see now how bitterness has tried to ruin my life and cause me to live with anger and unforgiveness. I also see how bitterness has tried to lead me to become more self-reliant and less dependent on you Lord. You said in Your Word that you came that we may "have life," and that we may "have it more abundantly" (John 10:10). Please restore me back to You, Lord. I surrender my will to You right now. Teach me how to profit from my pain and live life forward. Amen.*

Congratulations! Today is the start of a new, better chapter in your life. From this moment on, the past is the past; "old things are passed away...[and] all things are become new" (2 Cor. 5:17). In the pages that follow you will not only learn how to gain freedom from the spirit of bitterness, but you will also learn how to walk in this newfound freedom and relationship with Christ. Two of the most important elements of this process are accountability and spiritual community. If you do not already attend a church that teaches the Word of God, find one. Get involved in a small group there, and find an accountability partner of the same sex who is living their life in the Lord, someone you trust, who will be honest with you, and who will hold you responsible for your commitment to serving God and pursuing deliverance. There are also many ministries online who publish great resources that will help you mature in the things of God.

Now that you're ready to embark on the steps to uprooting the spirit of bitterness in your life, let's get started! The steps below are an overview of what we will cover in the following chapters in greater detail.

Step One: Acknowledge the true nature of bitterness

The first step in apprehending the silent killer is to acknowledge that bitterness isn't an emotional issue. Rather, it is a spirit oftentimes working within. I'll say it again: we must agree that the spirit of bitterness is more than a human emotion but rather a demonic spirit. Bitterness masquerades as an emotion, and it may seem a natural expression after a negative, traumatic experience. But in reality, it is nothing more than a spirit bent on deceiving the wounded and preying on their pain. We will continue to fight a losing battle as long as we are attempting to fight this spiritual battle with man-made weaponry. The Bible states, "For we are not fighting against people made of flesh and blood, but... evil rulers of the unseen world, those mighty satanic beings and great evil princes of darkness who rule this world; and against huge numbers of wicked spirits in the spirit world" (Eph. 6:12, TLB). To overcome this spirit, we must rely on the help of the Lord, the source of our freedom.

Step Two: Forgiveness

Forgiveness is the central theme of the Bible. The work of Jesus was all about restoring man back to God. This was accomplished through His life and His death, which He gave on behalf of mankind. As God extends forgiveness to man, mankind has a responsibility to first forgive himself for all the self-guilt that he maybe harboring and then forgive others. Elaine Walton, PhD, author of the article "The Role of Forgiveness in Healing Intimate Wounds," perfectly summarizes the role of forgiveness in gaining freedom from bitterness when she writes:

> Forgiveness has long been accepted as an important Christian principle (e.g., Matthew 6:14; Matthew 18:22). It has also been viewed as a central and necessary part of emotional healing (DiBlasio, 1993)....Moreover, Erikson (1950) considered forgiveness to be an integral part of human development toward maturation.[3]

The healing process can't start in a wounded, bitter person until forgiveness has been extended.

Step Three: Confrontation

Confrontation is essential in the healing process. It is actually therapeutic. To be able to face your abuser and release all the pent up frustration and pain is actually an act of releasing and unloading pent-up bitterness. If it is impossible to face the abuser, there is a practice that many employ. This practice—whether face-to-face or by proxy—informs the pain you are carrying that bitterness is longer welcome to live in your mind and heart.

Step Four: Extending grace

Extending grace is a supernatural act, especially to someone who has brought you harm and pain. It's only accomplished with the help of the Lord. When the abused person releases the weight of the offense to God, then God downloads the courage and strength needed to extend divine grace to the abuser. This process allows restoration to take place in the life of the bitter person and opens the door for healing within the person or persons who hurt them.

Step Five: Living in love

God has issued the body of Christ an imperative to love. It is essential according to the Word of God: "For this is the message that you heard from the beginning, that we should love one another" (1 John 3:11, NKJV). The Scriptures goes on to say acts of generosity without genuine love are nothing (1 Cor. 13:3, NKJV). Living in love is not pretending to not see the evil in people, but it is choosing to respond to what you see in a Christlike manner instead of taking offense or developing a victim mentality. This approach does not allow bitterness to penetrate your heart.

Step Six: Maintaining a heart of deliverance

Staying free from the spirit of bitterness is a lifelong pursuit. Just as alcoholics are often taught that they must keep the mind-set, even once sober, that they will always need to avoid alcohol to remain free from the grip of alcohol addiction, those who have harbored the spirit of bitterness must be vigilant every day against the attempts of the enemy to trick them into glorifying their emotions over the freedom God offers them through the process of forgiveness. Bitterness only manifests itself when a person who has been offended or wounded refuses to forgive the offender and continues to rehearse the issue, dwelling on the person who injured them. That's why the key to maintaining freedom is denying access to bitterness through extending forgiveness and living in love. This is done through the active choice of your will to reposition your thoughts from negative to productive thoughts. The wounded person must reposition the negative image, thought, or trauma to its proper place. Stop feeding it! Choose to move on. Choose to live life forward every single day.

———

Jesus states in 3 John 2, "My dear friend [Beloved], I pray that you are doing well [prospering] in every way [all respects] and that your health is good, just as your soul is doing fine [it is well with your soul; your soul is prospering]" (EXV). As we can see, the Jesus of the Bible desires is to see people whole and sound in every part of their makeup, having no trace of bitterness but living in love, prospering in their souls, and having a great outlook on life. He wants us living our lives forward, knowing that the spirit of bitterness has been apprehended.

You hold the keys. Lock bitterness up forever!

Chapter 7

GETTING TO THE BITTER ROOT

*Be careful what you think [Above all that
you guard, protect your heart], because your
thoughts run your life [life flows from it].*
—PROVERBS 4:23, EXV

IN TODAY'S WORLD, if one would stop and take a panoramic view of society, especially here in the United States; you would be able to see a great deal of carnage taking place within the streets and cities of this country. We see at times a great deal of lawlessness. Our youth today seem to be out of control. Drug use is growing. Even now states are beginning to succumb and give into the desires of hurting people by legalizing certain drugs. We even have television shows that highlight man's depravity. Many viewers are intrigued with the sin and dysfunction of reality shows stars. Sadly, many view these shows as a form of entertainment, but the question must be asked, "At what cost?" At someone else's misery and pain?

Our law enforcement officials are arresting people in

record numbers; however, many people have lost respect and belief in them because of numerous cases of officer abuse and corruption of their authority. Therefore, many people today are very leery, and there is a major trust issue with law enforcement officials.

These realities will cause many to examine only the fruit of a person's life. We often try to judge and treat dysfunctions within the fruit that we see, all the while neglecting the root of that tree. Physicians are confronted daily with the task of treating the manifestation of illness, but unless they take the time to go to the root of the problem, that person will continue to have recurring problems. If a person were to examine an onion that has been cut into two pieces, that person would then be able to see the countless numbers of layers within that onion. Nonetheless, there is an end to the countless number of layers, and that is called the core of the onion.

Man is very complex. Like the onion, he also has many layers to his makeup; however, at his core there is a center or a metaphorical root. Often the person that is suffering has refused to deal with the core of their issues, the origin of pain. The Bible tells us Jesus says, "Look! I have been standing at the door, and I am constantly knocking. If anyone hears me calling him and opens the door, I will come in and fellowship with him and he with me" (Rev. 3:20, TLB). Here Jesus is extending an invitation to all hurting people to come and discuss the issues of their life. He wants to have intimate fellowship with us to help restore us from our carnal and self-reliant mind-set back to a dependence on and desire for God, for His love, and for His presence. However, Jesus is unlike mental health counselors. They try to treat core issues, but when they are not successful at getting to the root, they will do nothing more that prescribe a medication. That temporarily anesthetizes the patient.

To get to the core of the bitter root, we first must know what to look for. Looking at the root system of a plant should help us to first identify the root and understand the purpose of the root, its function, and eventually eradicate the root. Plants' root systems include the following functions:

- Anchorage and support
- Absorption and conduction
- Storage
- Photosynthesis
- Aeration
- Movement
- Reproduction[1]

As we see, the root system is very critical in the survival of plant life. All of this important plant growth takes place out of sight, away from the naked eye.

Just as the plant root system anchors and supports

the stability of the plant, so do the hurt, pain, and unresolved offenses that are stored in a person's soul affect their stability and stature. Therefore, an excavation mission must take place, a mission that will go deep beneath the surface. This is a process that is aimed at excavating and unearthing all demonic support systems that help foster and support the spirit of bitterness. It not enough to cut the supply lines. A total removal of all foreign, poisonous roots must take place.

The Hebrews called the heart the *leb*, the emotional center of a human being.[2] That position metaphorically is in the center of the person's body.[3] The heart can experience varying emotions. The following scriptures describe which emotions the heart can experience.

> Emotionally, the heart experiences intoxicated merriment (1 Sm 25:36), gladness (Is 30:29), joy (Jn 16:22)...bitterness (Prv 14:10), anxiety (1 Sm 4:13)...love (2 Sm 14:1)...affection (2 Cor 7:3), lust (Mt 5:28)...hatred (Lv 19:17)...desire (Rom 10:1)... and much more.[4]

As we see, the heart is alive, and it appears to have a mind of its own! Anatomically, yes, its main function is to distribute blood to vital organs throughout the body, but God allows the reader of His Word to understand it is there within the heart where man determines how he will filter life's negative experiences. The person that is walking in bitterness, is walking in rebellion against God and His principles is often unaware that they are harboring bitterness because it's a deep, undercover work, a cooperative effort that is taking place within their heart.

The cooperative work is the constant attempt at imprisoning the person with demonic suggestions that attempt to entice the wounded person to listen and agree with the spirit of bitterness. This allows the roots of the silent killer to lodge themselves in a person's soul. When this happens, the silent killer begins killing the person emotionally, snuffing out vital emotions. The spirit of bitterness does not allow the person to live life forward but silently restricts and directs the person to live life in reverse, always wanting some type of retribution for past hurts and offenses. This person is now trapped in their personal closet of pain. Retaliation, unforgiveness, resentment, and bitterness are all just hanging up and waiting to be worn daily.

To stay committed to the path of gaining total freedom from the spirit of bitterness, you must understand and know your heart is valuable! According to Susan Thomas:

> We don't guard something that's worth nothing. When I take out my trash, I'm fine with walking away. As long as it's gone, I'm not too concerned with who comes and gets it. However, I would never intentionally leave my wedding ring sitting on the street corner or cash my paycheck and give it all to my five-year-old [sic] to play "store." When

something is valuable, we guard it. We protect it. Your heart is of huge value. And God says guard it![5]

Keeping guard, or watch over, our heart is critical to our mental stability. Arthur Fletcher, the former head of the United Negro College Fund, coined the well-known phrase, "A mind is a terrible thing to waste." The statement contains so much truth. The Bible also concurs with that statement: "For as he thinks in his heart, so is he" (Prov. 23:7, NKJV). The Bible and Mr. Arthur Fletcher are saying it is important what we allow to occupy our thoughts and minds. Constant negative thoughts of betrayal, rejection, and neglect causes people to live in a type of demonic loop. They are never taking any positive ground toward recovery and restoration. Highlighting the pain and memory of an offense will never help anybody move forward.

GOD AND THE BEGINNING—AND END—OF BITTERNESS

If you take all this into consideration, it is obvious that getting to the core of bitterness really means evaluating the condition of your heart and your mind. It's performing a heavenly MRI in order to detect any hatred, bitterness, and unforgiveness and access the damage sustained for many years. Once a person willfully undergoes the heavenly MRI test and finally admits it's been their stubbornness, their bullheads, and their inflexibility that has kept them in a self-imposed prison, then freedom is assured progressively.

The person must then undergo a heart transplant procedure, performed by the universally renowned master surgeon, Jesus Christ Himself! The goal of the transplant is the removal of the old, stony heart, with its sin nature, and replacing it with a new heart. At the same time the mind must be transformed to the mind of Christ. The Bible states God is willing and ready to perform this life-saving surgery. He promises, "I will give you a new heart, and I will put a new way of thinking [spirit] inside you. I will take out [remove from you] the stubborn hearts of stone from your bodies [your heart of stone], and I will give you obedient hearts [a heart] of flesh. I will put my Spirit [or spirit] inside you [or among you; the pronoun is plural] and help you [cause you] to live by [walk in] my rules [statutes] and carefully obey my laws [rules; judgments]" (Ezek. 36:26–27).

The God of the Bible says in Psalm 46:1 that He "is our protection [refuge] and our strength. He always helps [is an ever present/timely help] in times of trouble [distress]" (EXV). However, if a person sees their pain through blurred vision, it will often cause the individual to see the God of the Bible as a punisher instead of protector. Many bitter people never submit to this evaluation or receive this transformative transplant because they are angry with God. They feel that if God is real and is as all-powerful as the Bible claims, then why does He allow bad things to happen to good people? How can

He be trusted if He permitted the trauma that caused them so much pain? This misunderstanding of the nature of God and His role in our lives must be dealt with before any healing can take place.

Some say man is a free moral agent. That's not the total truth. In fact, J. Preston Eby explains the phrase "free moral agent" within his article "Just What Do You Mean Man Is a Free Moral Agent":

> Let me call attention to the fact that the phrase "free moral agent" is not a Scriptural one, any more than the term "rapture" is Scriptural. Free moral agency is simply a theological expression, manufactured for his own convenience, and like most human inventions, and extra-biblical terminology, is not the truth at all. But briefly let us examine these three words: free moral agent.
>
> 1. An *agent* is an actor, one who can act or perform.
> 2. A *free* agent is one who can act as he pleases without any restraint of any kind placed upon him.
> 3. A free *moral* agent is one who is free to act as he pleases and without any restraint on all moral issues, i.e., all questions involving the qualities of right and wrong.[6]

According to Wayne Jackson in his article titled "Does Free Agency Nullify Personal Responsibility?" "'Free agency' is not the *right* to do as one wishes. Rather, it is the *ability* to make choices, to decide between opposites. It involves the innate opportunity to exercise one's will to 'do' or 'not to do' something."[7] He further states:

> "Free agency" is a gift from God, bestowed as a part of that wonderful "package" of being created in his "image" (Gen. 1:26–27). It is an honor bestowed, allowing us the option of making responsible choices between good and evil. We do not deny that some environments may facilitate good or evil choices; nonetheless, such do not utterly negate human volition.[8]

From the statements above, we see the God of the Bible created man with the ability to choose to do good, but when man leaves godly character and yields to a sin nature he can and often does harm or evil. This doesn't make free agency any less a gift to mankind from God. Instead, it shows the goodness of God in granting that "honor" to man, as Jackson says, and underscores our profound need for His guidance.

The Bible states in John 16:33, "I told you these things so that you can have peace in me. In this world, you will have trouble [persecution; suffering], but be brave [take courage/heart]! I have defeated [victory over; conquered; overcome] the world" (EXV). This scripture reveals man is sure to be confronted with persecution (people trouble). The definition of *persecution*, taken from the Oxford Living Dictionary, is "hostility and ill-treatment, especially because of race or political or religious beliefs...a persistent annoyance or harassment."[9] It appears that mankind will be subjected to ill treatment, may it be physical or verbal. This information informs the man that being hurt is a part of living, but choosing whether or not to harbor the hurt makes all the difference in the world. This ill treatment gives man the chance, the opportunity, to choose to be angry or not. Anger is a human emotion. Allowing anger to build and fester creates a perfect incubator for bitterness to be nourished over the ill treatment or suffering received. Choosing to turn that anger over to the Lord so that He can heal and restore our heart is the better choice.

Don't forget we as humans all have a sin nature, and within that nature is the ability to seek revenge, harbor resentment, and grow the root of bitterness. Where did the sin nature come from? The Bible states man was made in His likeness, "in the image of God" (Gen. 1:27). However, Genesis records the disobedience of Adam and Eve and the entrance of rebellion against God. From generation to generation, the sin nature was passed down to all humanity. This continues to be the case with mankind today. A person who does not have a relationship with the God of the Bible and refuses to adhere to His tenets will both cause others pain and filter offenses in an anti-God manner. Why is this? According to the Bible, "A person who does not have the Spirit [or natural person] does not accept the truths [things] that come from the Spirit of God. That person thinks they are foolish and cannot understand them, because they can only be judge to be true [discerned; assessed] by the Spirit" (1 Cor. 2:14, ESV).

So, is the answer to just accept Jesus Christ and Lord and Savior? That's a great first step, but salvation alone doesn't eradicate the root of bitterness. The truth of the matter is accepting Jesus into your heart and receiving that heavenly heart transplant does not remove the sin nature; instead, it frees you from its authority over your life and grants you power through the Spirit to overcome that nature. The Apostle Paul gave a startling discourse on the pull of the two natures housed within his being:

> [For] I do not understand the things I do. [For] I do not do what I want to do, and I do the things I hate. And if I do what I do not want to do, that means I agree that the law is good [Paul's acknowledgement that his behavior is wrong confirms the law's righteous standards]. But [now] I am not really the one who is doing these hated things; it is sin living in me that does them. Yes [For...], I know that nothing good lives in me—I mean nothing good lives in ·the part of me that is earthly and sinful [my sinful self; my sinful nature; my flesh]. [For] I want to do the things that are good, but I do not [or cannot] do them.
>
> —ROMANS 7:15–18, EXV

As we see from this scripture, Paul tells all potential followers of God that just because someone pledges allegiance to God, it does not insulate them from reverting to the sin nature, thus becoming bitter over an offense and solidifying the grip of the silent killer.

It is a choice to stay rooted in God instead of rooted in bitterness! The Christian is directed to walk in the Spirit and live their Christian life in the spirit. This allows the Christian to live above his situation and circumstances. This allows the person to live above the offense and not rehearse the painful incident repeatedly. Their hope comes from the hope and glory of being in Christ and understanding God's will for their lives.

> To them God willed to make known what are
> the riches of the glory of this mystery among the
> Gentiles, which is Christ in you, the hope of glory.
> —COLOSSIANS 1:27, NKJV

Those who chose to walk [live] in the Spirit will show forth progress in the holiness that God desires for their lives. This progress is essential to removing the root of the spirit of bitterness. The person that is allowing bitterness to hurt them is living in their senses; therefore, you must understand, if a person chooses to live a Christian life and be successful they must learn to mortify their senses:

> Likewise, you also, reckon yourselves to be dead
> indeed to sin but alive to God in Christ Jesus our

Lord. Therefore, do not let sin reign in your mortal
body, that you should obey it in its lusts....For sin
shall not have dominion over you, for you are not
under law but under grace.

—ROMANS 6:11–12, 14, NKJV

The Bible is simply stating, don't choose to live in bitterness because it is sin! Yes, the offense was wrong and
painful; however, don't choose to harbor the silent killer.
It will cause you to sin and bring more frustration and
pain, along with possible damaging side effects to your
body! Boot out the silent killer and destroy its root so
that you can get rid of it for good!

DESTROYING THE ROOT FOR GOOD

Are you ready to submit to the Lord and allow Him to
lead you in the process of eradicating the spirit of bitterness from your life? If so, pray this prayer with me
before you move on to the next chapter—and the next
stage in your journey toward total freedom.

*The Word of God states in 2 Timothy 1:7, "For
God did not give us a spirit of timidity or cow-
ardice or fear, but [He has given us a spirit]
of power and of love and of sound judgment
and personal discipline [abilities that result
in a calm, well-balanced mind and self-con-
trol] (AMP). Therefore, I choose to forge forward with God, understanding He holds me
and that any attacks of retaliation from the*

enemy and any negative memory recall will neither hinder me nor prosper against me. Understanding this, I will not walk in timidity. Though I realize that eradicating the bitterness in my life may cause me some sort of discomfort, I choose to trust God. Amen.

Chapter 8

FORGIVE

Be kind and loving [compassionate; ten-
derhearted] to each other, and forgive each
other just as God forgave you in Christ.
—EPHESIANS 4:32, ESV

ANY PEOPLE TODAY are angry with other people who have hurt, abused, offended, or injured them physically—and rightfully so. But, because the war against the spirit of bitterness is a spiritual battle, we must battle in the spirit. This means our real battle is against spiritual forces, not with the person who was the agent of pain, the one that carried out the demonic deed. The Bible states, "For we are not wrestling against flesh-and-blood enemies, but against evil rulers and authorities of the unseen world, against mighty powers in this dark world, and against evil spirit in the heavenly places" (Eph. 6:12, NLT). Reading this scripture reminds us to remain alert and vigilant! The ruler of demonic spirits, the devil himself, is on the loose and like a lion seeking his next piece of prey. It also instructs us that holding grudges against human enemies and refusing to forgive is ultimately fruitless. It will only result in our own destruction, and the devil knows it.

We must understand that the spirit of bitterness has an agenda. It has an agenda to destroy your life and those you care about. It wants to isolate you from the Lord and from vital relationships that will help you heal by causing you to see them as enemies instead of sources of provision and blessing. We have learned that any person who is harboring bitterness is a person who will eventually spiral out of control emotionally and implode. This is a person who will find themselves in a losing battle if they continue to harbor resentment. The Bible states that the devil wants to confuse your natural thinking. It may seem natural to hold grudges, have resentment, and harbor bitterness in our heart. However, this is not what God intended when He created us in His likeness.

Many people convince themselves they have valid reasons not to entertain the thought of forgiveness. Some have lived through horrendous atrocities. Some have lost property, jobs, and material possessions—all of which can be replaced. Then there are those who have been the victims of personal abuse. These are the types of losses some people find are impossible to get over. Naturally, some say time heals all wounds, but many have lived long enough to know that is not exactly true. There are people that have been abused, raped, been victims of domestic violence, victims of horrendous crimes that took place twenty years or more ago, but these same people are still reeling and suffering from their pain. So, they find themselves medicating, attending secular self-help groups, or turning their pain on someone else and using them to vent or as a punching bag.

Nevertheless, there is good news today. The God of the Bible wants the bitter person to take the high road and has made that action possible. He says, "Simply forgive and free yourselves!" For some that seems easier said than done, but it is essential, and with God's help, it is possible for everyone.

SUPERNATURAL FORGIVENESS

We must understand that forgiveness is not an innate response that humans possess or often display. Forgiveness is not automatically in our nature. The act of forgiveness is something that is foreign; therefore, it is a learned behavior and must be embraced before it can be then displayed inwardly and outwardly.

Genuine forgiveness does not find its origin in the realm of Earth! Genuine forgiveness is a divine attribute from a divine being. Forgiveness is from another dimension beyond man's mental comprehension. It does not come from knowledge acquired from a book or from another person. The act of forgiveness originates from the Creator of the universe, from Elohim—God himself! According to the Bible, God did not just define forgiveness but exemplified it in action: "For God so loved the world, that he gave his only begotten son, that whosever believeth in him should not perish, but have everlasting life" (John 3:16). For forgiveness to have any merit or power at all, we should acknowledge it as a godly act. Consequently, without a genuine, intimate relationship with God it is almost impossible to understand genuine forgiveness and embody it, let alone extend forgiveness and truly mean it.

According to the *Tyndale Bible Dictionary*, *forgiveness* is defined as "a pardon, involving restoration of broken relationships; cease to feel resentment for wrongs and offenses."[1] Forgiveness is also a human act extended toward ones neighbor a manifestation of realization and appropriation of God forgiveness. Hence, forgiveness is a uniquely Christian doctrine. Psychologists generally define *forgiveness* as "a conscious, deliberate decision to release feelings of resentment or vengeance toward a person or group who has harmed you, regardless of whether they actually deserve your forgiveness."[2] As we can see, forgiveness is an action word that requires the person extending forgiveness to release, pardon, and wipe away the offense and no longer hold hateful resentment toward the offending party.

It is almost always very difficult to release an offender. We subconsciously want the offender to experience some type of retribution for their offenses. Many people refuse to extend forgiveness because of the nature of the offense.

That's why man's forgiveness is limited and has conditions attached to it. This can be seen in our criminal justice system here in the United States. There are certain crimes for which after an offender serves his or her punishment he or she is released and can resume some type of normalcy to their life. Then there are crimes for which even after serving the penalty time the individual is released but has limited access, mobility, privileges, and rights. Their life is scrutinized and monitored. So it is with man's forgiveness. Certain types of offenses we are unwillingly to forgive; therefore, we give people limited pardons with limited access and mobility back into our lives. We look at them with cautious, distrustful, and leery eyes, all the while wondering if there is a hidden agenda within their corrupt soul.

This type of forgiveness is fleeting at best. When the offender reoffends the victim, the victim explodes like a volcanic eruption. All types of pent-up feelings come spewing out and up to the surface like lava. These feelings contaminate anyone listening or viewing the eruption. The eruption causes old keloids to be ripped open viciously once again and unhealed, stinking, festering wounds to worsen! Because of conditional forgiveness, the recidivism rate is high and expected, and thus bitterness remains the silent killer still on the loose.

Bitterness and forgiveness are both mental states that we choose to arrive at. Bitterness is fueled by unforgiveness, while forgiveness is fueled by love. Bitterness bleeds poison into our souls and infects us spiritually, while forgiveness unlocks the door to hatred so that it can leave and no longer torment us.

For forgiveness to be genuine and transformative it must be motivated by love. Robert Muller wrote, "To forgive is the highest, most beautiful form of love. In return you will receive untold peace and happiness."[3] There must be an exchange that is forthcoming in which bitterness is released and joy is embraced. This can only happen when a person has embraced and applied biblical principles. The releasing of bitterness and embracing of joy is tied to being Christ like.

A perfect picture of this can be seen in the Bible in the parable of the lost son. Jesus' words tell the story of the older brother and his feelings of bitterness toward his young brother. Jesus tells us that instead of embracing his father's decision to forgive and receive the prodigal son back home, the older brother bitterly accused his father of wasting his wealth on a lost cause: "But as soon as this son of yours came, who has devoured your livelihood with harlots, you killed the fatted calf for him" (Luke 15:30). We see that the father's loving response to his lost son contrasts the older brother's bitterness. The father forgave because he was filled with love, but the older brother was filled with resentment; therefore, he was unable and unwilling to make the transition from bitterness to joy to forgiveness.

This parable perfectly demonstrates how bitterness blinds, blocks, and prevents a person from receiving revelation about their situation and any possible strategy for breakthrough. When a person's vision is blurred, they tend to display characteristics of a person suffering from self-pity. When a person is consumed by self-pity, they play the blame game about who hurt them. At this point, the individual is experiencing a form of arrested development. When a new trauma or offense occurs, the person is stuck in that place emotionally and cannot progress forward past the hurt or offense. In the parable of the lost son, the older brother continued to place blame on his younger brother, and then on his father, instead of admitting to and dealing with his own bitterness. He acted like a petulant child so hung up on his younger brother's past behavior—from which his brother had repented—that he couldn't perceive how immaturely he was acting.

Perhaps he found it hard to forgive his brother, as their father had done, because he was unwilling to forget his brother's actions. This may be an unpopular statement, but true forgiveness may mean forgetting the wrong committed against you. This is without a doubt a very controversial statement, and many may not agree with me. However, we as humans must have some type of standard or code we choose to follow. And that standard should be able to tell us how we should filter life's positive as well as negative experiences. If you are a Christian and say you are living according to biblical statutes and standards, you should be modeling God's way of handling problems. Psalm 103:12 states, "As far as the east is from the west, So far has He removed our transgressions from us" (NKJV). We see from this statement that God separates the offense from the offender, and He no longer holds our sins over our head. If we are going to truly forgive our abuser, we can't continue to run the offense on a continuous loop in our mind and expect to forgive the person and not harbor any ill feelings toward them. It's impossible!

Some may say they will never choose to forget; therefore, they have resolved just to keep their feelings of bitterness toward their abuser and allow the silent killer to have a field day in their lives. Unbeknownst to them, their decision not to forget means they are saying, "I am willing to allow the silent killer to wreak havoc in my soul, and I will live with whatever residual effects of bitterness it may cause me."

These same people often cry out from their heart, "I refuse to be a weak person!" As youths, many are told that respect a form of protection, and forgiveness is perceived as weakness. They are taught to protect themselves and that if someone injures them they should retaliate to gain respect. This is why many youths are taught you don't want to be soft or be a pushover. They never want to feel weak or be hurt again, nor do they want to be disrespected, so they choose to be unforgiving and hard hearted. This is part of the cause of the epidemic of unforgiveness, but it is also one of the reasons we have so many killings of young people on our streets today in this country. Where you grow up and whom you spend quality years around does have the ability to plant seeds of love, joy, and peace or seeds of resentment and bitterness in your life.

The truth is, forgiveness demonstrates strength, not weakness! Deciding if a person is worthy of forgiveness is an extremely difficult decision to make. In some instances it may be relatively easy to forgive once you make the decision to do so, but in other instances it may take significant prayer and total, complete surrender to the Lord. If someone stole something from you and planned to have you killed at the first available chance, would this person be worthy of forgiveness? What if someone actually killed a person you loved? If it were within your powers and authority, would you forgive him or her? Would the decision to forgive in this instance demonstrate weakness or strength? To answer this question we must go back to a person's value system. What would the Bible say? If this is to be your life's standard, your decision must match up with Christ's; that is what it means to walk in Christlikeness. Does your value system vacillate like many average man-made systems? Does your belief system leave room for repentance, forgiveness, and restoration?

A BIBLICAL MODEL FOR UNCONDITIONAL FORGIVENESS

You must have the mind-set to forgive regardless of the circumstances. As we see, the act of forgiving someone is critical. Naomi needed to forgive several people before she could ever receive restoration to her wounded and bitter soul. As we saw in the last chapter, the first person Naomi had to forgive was God. It was not God's fault for the calamity that hit her life. The Scriptures tell us in no uncertain terms that we live in the aftermath of our own decisions. Even though she lived in a male-dominated society where women had little or no voice in important matters, she was married, and God viewed Naomi and Elimelech as one.

That leads to the next individual she had to forgive: herself. Naomi had to acknowledge that her God, the God her culture served, saw married couples as one flesh according to Genesis 2:24 (NIV). When married couples today have issues within the marriage, and even if one is to blame for the problems within the union, God views the couple as one. Therefore, there was some accountability on her part. Her role in the decision to leave Bethlehem, no matter how large or small, must still be acknowledged. She was also responsible for allowing bitterness to take root in her heart and for assuming it as her identity. Every believer is equally responsible for resisting the whispers of the enemy.

Certainly one of the hardest people to forgive would have been her deceased husband. That's right, Naomi had to face the fact that it was Elimelech's idea and final decision to leave Bethlehem for the country of Moab. Leaving was supposed to be for the family security and survival. However, her husband's decision also meant she was leaving a closely knit society where she had significance, she knew her place, and had comradery with the other women of her community. As we have discussed, it is common for people to hold grudges toward someone who might have been the initiator of their pain. However, if the person has transitioned out of this world and on to the next, the bitter person should not take the attitude "out of sight, out of mind." If this approach is taken, there will yet remain unresolved pain in their heart and confusion in their mind, which will contaminate their spirit.

Once Naomi forgave God, her deceased husband, and herself, it allowed bitterness to be released out of her spirit. Finally she stood ready to receive healing, mercy, and restoration from God's hand. This happens as Naomi intentionally chooses to forgive all the parties in her painful story. Have you forgiven all the parties in your story, starting with forgiving God, your offender[s], and yourself?

The story of Joseph is a very intriguing and compelling story about a young man who was treated very cruelly by his siblings. They tried to kill him and sold him into slavery to live a harsh life filled with possible abuse, ill treatment, and misery. From the outside, this young man's life seemed to be spiraling downward; however, the God of the Bible was positioning him for promotion, success, wealth, and authority. Joseph's path to abundance and authority came after taking one of the longest, most circuitous routes in human history. This young man living in slavery never thought his life would amount to anything under the conditions that he was in. He had absolutely no control over his future; however, he did have control over his now!

Joseph decided to forgive his siblings, not knowing that he would ever see them again. The story can be found in Genesis 37, 39–50. At the pinnacle of his power, with no restraints to hold him back, Joseph extended the olive branch of forgiveness and did not succumb to the suggestions of the silent killer whispering in his ear telling him to get bitter and get revenge! When the appropriate time presented itself, Joseph explained to his brothers, "But as for you, you meant evil against me; but God meant it for good, in order to bring it about as it is this day, to save many people alive" (Gen. 50:20, NKJV). Not only did Joseph forgive them, but he used his newfound authority and power to provide for them instead of using that power and authority to hurt them (Gen. 45:10–11).

So how did Joseph choose forgiveness over bitterness? We must understand it was a process for Joseph to extend forgiveness, as it is for anyone on the road to eradicating the spirit of bitterness from their life. After the decision to choose to forgive, it's time to:

1. Acknowledge the hurt.

Deliberately avoiding the pain that surrounds an event is never good idea. Not acknowledging the hurt or offense won't and can't prepare a person to forgive the person who injured them.

2. Understand forgiveness is not the same as denial.

Denial says no hurt ever took place. That untruth delays healing and restoration and does not allow both parties to forgive and be healed property. Forgiveness allows you as the forgiver to separate the offense from the person and concentrate on forgiving the person.

3. Don't just suppress the pain.

Speak about your pain. Allow the abuser to know they hurt you and to look at your pain. (We will discuss this further in the next chapter.) Tell your pain you choose to remove it from your life forever.

4. Realize that out of sight is not out of mind.

Remember, distance from the abuser—geographically or time-wise—is not the same as forgiving them: Some people who may have hurt us are dead and gone or simply out of our sphere of contact. Does that mean we will not be able to get relief? Not so! Joseph forgave his brothers, not knowing that he would ever see them again.

Conduct an exercise where you place the abuser in a chair in front of you. Once you can visualize the person in this imaginary chair, vent out everything you always wanted to say, and after this venting session release the person and free yourself.

Why should this be done? You are attempting to free yourself emotionally and eradicate any root of bitterness, and you cannot do this without dealing with the source of the hurt. Also, we have a biblical mandate to forgive unconditionally: "Be kind to one another, tenderhearted, forgiving one another, even as God in Christ forgave you" (Eph. 4:32, NKJV).

5. Extend grace.

There is no guarantee in forgiving the abuser. You need to know some people will never apologize for their actions. Your decision to forgive does not mean the person or people who hurt you will accept your forgiveness. They may not even want your forgiveness. Don't expect the abuser to feel the way you are now feeling. Don't allow their attitude to bring you back to a state of bitterness. Remember, God forgave us based on His grace and not our works, and He is our model. (This is the topic of chapter 10. We will deal with this topic in greater detail there.)

6. Maintain your freedom.

Stay committed to the process of extending unconditional forgiveness and eradicating the root of bitterness from your life at all costs. Even if you experience new rejection, offense, injury, or some other type of trauma, work to keep your heart pure. Forgive and start expecting supernatural breakthrough to come to you soon. Joseph realized God is omniscient and that He was aware of his situation and pain. Joseph concluded bitterness and unforgiveness were not acceptable in his life. He chose to maximize his today and trust the God of the Bible to turn his situation around without holding God to a time limit.

Remember that when you are offended, abandoned, injured, rejected, not affirmed, not supported, or not loved, your emotional and mental stability stand in the balance. You decide which way the pendulum swings—and stays. Apostle John Eckhardt writes, "Sometimes you have to stop and ask, why was I rejected [offended, injured]?"[4] Using discernment when you've been rejected (or offended or injured) can bring great deliverance and breakthrough to your life and to those around you, just as it did for Joseph. Remember:

- Forgiveness is tied to our healing (2 Chron. 7:14; Matt. 9:2–5).

- Forgiveness is tied to forgiving iniquities (Jer. 31:34; 36:3)

- Forgiveness is tied to releases us from debt (Matt. 6:12).

WE FORGIVE BECAUSE WE ARE FORGIVEN

Forgiveness is a hurdle that this country's citizens continue to have trouble getting over. Many people chose to be stuck and inflexible. They refuse to understand we all will be offended, hurt, and wounded at one time or another in our lives. We must remember that we determine how we will respond to the offense. We are responsible if we choose to be bitter and to place blame on ourselves or others, and we determine to extended forgiveness or not. However, for those who have been called to Christianity and have accepted the call, there is a higher standard that must be adhered to if you are going to remain in compliance with the Word of God. The Bible states, "For if you forgive men their trespasses, your heavenly Father will also forgive you. But if you do not forgive men their trespasses, nether will your Father forgive your trespasses" (Matt. 6:14–15, NKJV).

These verses present a dilemma. The abused, inevitably, one day, will rub someone else the wrong way intentionally or unintentionally. Either way, this person will also want to be forgiven for their actions and deeds. Remember, you reap what you sow, more than you sow, and later than you sow.[5] The Bible states, "Bearing with one another, and forgiving one another, if anyone has a complaint against another; even as Christ forgave you, so you also must do" (Col. 3:13, NKJV). We are called to forgive according to the model of Christ. He forgave us, so we must extend forgiveness to others. The Christian is called to accountability with their Christianity.

Now, some may say, "I am not a practicing Christian, so I am absolved from forgiving people that hurt me." They may claim it's alright to hold some grudges and be bitter. This line of reasoning may make sense to some people. They may be able to rationalize their lack of forgiveness and abundance of bitterness. But in the final analysis, what is their bitterness and lack of forgiveness producing? What type of fruit is their personal tree bearing? How is their stance helping to enrich the world? And what is the result of harboring the silent killer of bitterness in their heart? Death. Bitterness can only produce death.

Forgiveness is one of the central themes of the Bible, therefore forgiveness is a big deal! And, it's a big deal to God! With forgiveness, I do not just mean man forgiving man for offenses, injuries, and all types of atrocities but God extending His forgiveness to forgive man for all his sins, past, present, and future. Once again, forgiveness is a big deal to God! It cost God mightily to extend forgiveness, therefore it would behoove man to be more respectful toward God and acknowledge what He did on behalf of mankind. This respect may be seen by adhering to and displaying a godly mind-set and lifestyle.

> For God so loved the world that He gave His only begotten Son, that whoever believes in Him should not perish but have everlasting life.
> —JOHN 3:16, NKJV

We see that God sacrificed His Son to redeem (buy back) man so that he could become acceptable once again to a holy, pure, and righteous God. It is Him "in whom we have redemption through His blood, the forgiveness of sins" (Col. 1:14, NKJV). God used the costliest currency in the universe to pardon man and reunite with him. We know that bitterness can only produce death, but the antidote, the forgiveness of the Father, produces eternal life.

How often does God want people to forgive one another? Jesus told Peter to forgive "not up to seven times, but seventy times seven" (Matt. 18:21, AMP). Jesus was saying we should have a mind-set to forgive people continuously. We must never get to the point where we say, "Enough is enough. No more forgiveness; only revenge." If God is our model for forgiveness, and His capacity to forgive is limitless, there should never be a limit to our willingness to extend forgiveness.

The Christian faith is all about what God did for mankind to destroy the enmity that existed between God and man. He allowed the Son of man, Jesus Christ, to be sacrificed on behalf of man to restore our relationship with Him. If anyone had a good reason to be bitter and unforgiving, it was Jesus. He was arrested on trumped-up charges, taken to a kangaroo court at night, had no legal representation, and was accused of charges against the state without proof. False witnesses were gathered together to assassinate His character and He was beaten by guards repeatedly, with no camcorder to record the arrest. He was held that night without bail and in the morning taken to a regional governing magistrate to be tried. The magistrate wanted to release Him because of insufficient evidence, but because of fear for his job and political pressure from the corrupt church leaders of that day the magistrate attempted to pacify the jealously insecure church leaders. He allowed Jesus to be beaten, but the sadistic guards went overboard with the beating. Only God was keeping Him alive at that point. Pilate knew that the jealous leaders were threatened by Jesus and His sudden rise to fame. Nonetheless, because of the continuous pressure by the mob and the corrupt leaders, he yielded to their demands to have Him crucified. Instead of standing his ground as magistrate and telling the ravenous crowd he would release Jesus, he succumbed to the pressure and sentenced Him to death row.

The crucifixion was to take place at once! Crucifixion was the most barbaric form of execution of its day. The pain is unimaginable, the death painful and slow. Jesus was beaten past human recognition and hung between two thieves. However, Jesus showed His integrity because there was a need yet to be addressed. He stopped and asked His Father, out loud, to forgive His abusers, for they were ignorant and did not know what they were doing. Even in His final moments He left no chance for bitterness to creep into His heart. He asked God not to hold their actions against them. Through Christ's work on the cross two thousand years ago, Father God is telling bitter hearts today to stop holding it against your abuser. He says, "Release them to Me and choose to forgive, like my Jesus did."

> My friends, do not try to punish others when they
> wrong you [take revenge; avenge yourselves], but
> wait for God to punish them with his anger [leave

room for (God's) wrath]. [For] It is written: "·I will punish those who do wrong [Vengeance is mine]; I will repay them [Deut. 32:35]," says the Lord.
—ROMANS 12:19, EXV

Forgiveness is a choice. What will you choose? Will you pray the following prayer with me?

Father God, I come to You in need of strength and guidance. Your Word states in 2 Corinthians 5:17, "If anyone is in Christ, he is a new creation; old things have passed away; behold, all things have become new" (NKJV). Therefore, as a new creature in Christ, I need not to practice old coping mechanisms when it comes to when I have been offended or hurt. Lord, help me to list the people I believe have wounded me. Allow me to write the names down. Once this is done, give me the strength to release each person who has hurt and wounded me. Do not allow me to sabotage my own life because of a refusal to forgive the people who have hurt me. Lord, please forgive me for misplacing blame onto You, and show me how to forgive myself. Amen.

Chapter 9

CONFRONTED

Be angry and do not sin; do not let the
sun go down on your anger.
—EPHESIANS 4:26, ESV

U NRESOLVED ANGER OR pain does nothing more than fester and grow worse. Like a wound that is not cleaned out properly, once a little external pressure is applied to the scar tissue, the old pain comes rushing back into today's reality. Forgiveness helps close the wound, but confrontation is a crucial step in completing the healing process. Unless a person is willing to confront the ghost of their past (or their present tormentor) and acknowledge they have been hurt, injured, or wounded, that person will remain emotionally stuck. Their wounds will remain painful. Further, the offender or abuser will go on to wound others.

We live in a society where pleasure seeking is at an all-time high. This society spends billions of dollars annually trying to escape reality, trying to grasp all the feel-good life that they can. We do all we can to distance

ourselves from uncomfortable situations and environ-
ments. Anything or any person that brings any type of
discomfort or negativity we try to avoid. Sadly, in our
society the word *confrontation* has negative images
attached to it; therefore, people go to great lengths to
avoid being confronted or simply to avoid confrontations altogether.

Unfortunately, we live in a politically correct society, a
society where we are careful to gloss over issues that are
affecting people in a hurtful and negative way. When
problems are not addressed at all, or not addressed
properly, they tend to cause hurting people to react in a
disruptive manner.

When blatant sin is not confronted and addressed
properly, that sin will continue to impact people in a
negative way.

Is Confrontation Really Necessary?

It can be very difficult to confront the person who
hurt you and reveal to that person all the pain he or
she caused you. However painful, you must muster up
enough courage to face the person(s) who hurt you, or
you run the risk of never truly getting the relief that you
so desperately long for. For survivors whose offender
has died or moved away, the process of confrontation
may need to happen by proxy in order to release your
bottled-up frustration and pain, but the exercise is
essential nonetheless. In these cases it is helpful to seek

the counsel of a trusted Christian counselor, pastor, or other skilled mentor.

Knowing this, why do so many people forgo the chance to confront the person who injured them? There is an old saying that says those whose lives are ruled by fear ironically avoid what is necessary to remove it. In spite of the negative result, avoidance seems to be somewhat of a default for certain people. Many people are avoiders, but none more than a religious person. Fear is the real culprit when it comes to avoidance.[1] Fearful people avoid going to the doctor. Fear causes a person not to go to church. Fear causes a husband or wife to avoid confronting their spouse when they behave immorally. Fear causes a person to put up with and avoid dealing with a relative's alcoholism. Fear causes people to avoid confronting someone who hurt them, even though it is essential for their healing. As we can see, fear is at the root of avoidance. The Bible states, "For God has not given us a spirit of fearfulness, but one of power, love, and sound judgement" (2 Tim. 1:7, HCSB). God does not want fear to hold us back from walking in freedom and wholeness.

Others still avoid confrontation because at their core they are still angry and dissociated mentally from the event. Here are some good questions to ask to determine if this is the case: Does your mood swing severely when you think about the traumatic event? Are you suffering from post-traumatic stress disorder (PTSD) and shame? Have you succumbed to self-destructive behavior to escape the painful memory of the event? Are you living with major trust issues? If the answer is yes, it is likely you need to continue to work on turning the experience and hurt over to the Lord and finishing the process of forgiving all those who you perceive as responsible. You see, bitterness will often cause a person to be sharp and aggressive with everyone but the abuser. Becoming angry over an offense is natural. Anger is a natural response reaction that every human being possesses. However, people must become more responsible with their anger and control any negative reaction that they may display in conjunction with being angry, and they must not allow it to prevent them from extending total forgiveness and confronting the one who hurt them. It's OK to be angry over the offense, injury, or wound, but don't add insult to injury by sinning and becoming bitter. Bitter people often will not allow themselves to confront the abuser and become free; they are too busy being consumed and blinded by their own bitterness.

If we break down the word *confrontation* we may see confronting a subject in a different light.

> The prefix *con* means "together" or "with," and the root *fron* means "face; to stand or meet face to face." Confrontation is simply the act of coming face to face to resolve an issue.[2]

Being able to face the person who has caused you pain often is frightening, but at the same time it can be therapeutic, and it is necessary.

I believe many people have a problem with confronting the abuser simply because they have not settled on what is the best approach to take. Many people have expectations about an impending meeting and how the meeting should flow. Unfortunately, many of those same people have an unrealistic expectation in their minds.

First and foremost, many of these meetings are often very touchy and awkward at best. I look at my own life and when I had the opportunity to confront an absentee parent, one who had never been instrumental in any part of my life. It was very strange to say the least. Preparing to meet the person who was supposed to father me, protect me, mentor me, and provide for me—but did none of these things—was uncomfortable. There were many things I had dreamt of saying for years, things that would somehow tear him down, make him feel guilty and somewhat remorseful. Like many others in my place, I was waiting for him to apologize and take responsibility for his actions, words, or deeds. I wanted him to acknowledge his wrong behavior and understand that his absence caused me to harbor bitterness for years. The internal turmoil over these expectations caused tremendous pain and confusion. I wish I had known then what I know now about forgiveness and confrontation. These steps would have made my path to healing quicker and easier.

Still, it's important to remember that even when you are doing things 100 percent correctly, confrontation still takes total dependence on the leading of the Holy Spirit to get it right, and even then you may still perceive the flesh and the enemy trying to hijack the exchange. Unfortunately, this is not Hollywood, nor is this a feature film. This is real life! That's why you should approach any confrontation of this kind with a plan. Lay out your pain and how the abuser caused the bitterness. If your motive for confronting the abuser is to bring restoration and closure, your words must be carefully crafted and non-threatening. If you are expecting any type of dialogue, try to avoid words that incite additional conflict. You should also set expectations. Is this a one-time meeting because the injuries were so egregious that restoration is impossible? Or is restitution and restoration of relationship the primary purpose of confronting the person? If the goal of the confrontation is to have the person back in your life playing a prominent role, there will be additional meetings needed, and a mediator would be beneficial. They will aid in helping to unearth any potential landmines that could potentially disrupt or destroy the relationship altogether.

One of the first steps that must take place as you prepare for a confrontation like this is to remove all mental distractions, especially negative memory recall. Distractions help in the procrastination process, which prevents a person who is bitter from ever getting to a place where confrontation is possible. I am not saying pretend that the offense never happened, but allow yourself to acknowledge it and forge toward this all-important, liberating meeting.

Another hindrance to confrontation is licking or pacifying wounds of hurt. Choose to stop strengthening the bitter wound. Decide not to keep the wounds raw anymore. Desire, crave healing and wholeness and make strides to achieving it. Unfortunately, some people have learned to be identified with the abuse that they have suffered. Some people have subconsciously labeled themselves as victims; they are personified the abuse and become some type of poster child for assault. This does nothing more than keep bitterness alive and never allows the person to develop the courage needed to confront their situation and seek relief. Choose not to protect bitterness. Learn from offenses. Profit from the pain that you have endured. Choose to re-engage life and face all the ugly moments.

CONFRONTATION GOD'S WAY

In Galatians 2:11–21, we find the story where Paul calls the apostle Peter a hypocrite. Paul publicly rebuked Peter because of his hypocrisy of eating with Gentiles when it was convenient for him to do so but avoiding them at other times for fear of being ostracized by certain Jewish leaders for his association with them. No doubt Peter could have said within himself, "I will choose to be offended. My ego has been bruised," but he said, "Paul is right, and I'm wrong. Therefore, I must display maturity." He allowed the rebuke, acknowledged his hypocrisy, and didn't get bitter. Instead, he got better.

Their exchange teaches us a few things about confrontation, even though Paul was not confronting Peter because of a need to forgive and release Peter from some wrongdoing. It is an important model because it demonstrates a constructive confrontation that brought a Christlike resolution to the situation instead of harm to Peter's emotions. First and foremost, it makes it clear that if confrontation is ever going to work properly, it must contain several components. The first is love. Is our plan for confrontation motivated by love, as Paul's was? It must be, in order to be effective.

If you are confronting someone who has hurt you, you must ensure you have forgiven them completely before initiating a confrontation. Without the peace of total, unconditional, godly forgiveness, that confrontation could be tainted. Love is the most important aspect of confrontation, but it cannot coexist with unforgiveness and bitterness. Jeremiah 17:9–10 (EXV) says:

> More than anything else [Above all things], ·a person's mind is evil [the heart is deceitful; the heart is devious/crooked] and ·cannot be healed [desperately wicked; it is perverse/sick]. Who can ·understand [know] it? But I, the Lord, ·look into a person's [investigate/test the] heart and test the ·mind [kidneys]. ·So I can decide what each one deserves [to give to each according to his way/

path]; I can give each one the right payment for
what he does.

It is our role to be emissaries of His love by extending
forgiveness and confronting sin lovingly, as Christ did.

It is not our job to tattle on people or develop a hier-
archy of who is better than whom based on actions. The
Lord knows "what each one deserves" (v. 10). Yes, there
are people who will hurt and offend you. And yes, there
are demonic forces using people to harm others, but
remember, we have a proper role to play in the exchange
of offender and offended, and our role is to act in love.

The apostle Paul knew that he had to confront the
apostle Peter before his actions damaged the church. So,
Paul brought the hypocrisy to Peter's attention. Even
Christian leaders make mistakes, and Paul's humility in
admitting his own shortcomings (Rom 7:18–20, 24–25)
gives evidence to the loving motive of his heart.

The second component of confrontation is confronting
with a motive of forgiving. This will allow the person to
understand you forgive and release them from this debt
to seek revenge. We must follow the model of Christ,
who bore the cost of our sins—even those sins committed against Him—when He pardoned us; in doing
so, He made reconciliation possible. Our willingness to
extend forgiveness in confrontation similarly opens the
door to reconciliation and restoration. However, you
must understand that this step is not about the abuser
accepting your forgiveness; it's about you releasing

them from the act, behavior, or other harm that left you wounded.

The third component is caring. If you truly love or care about a person, you must correct him or her if given the opportunity. If correction is needed, it must not be withheld. The Bible gives an example of this in the Book of 2 Corinthians. There you read of the apostle Paul anguishing in mental pain before he wrote his second letter to the Corinthian church to correct their behavior. He says, "For out of much affliction and anguish of heart I wrote to you, with many tears, not that you should be grieved, but that you might know the love which I have so abundantly for you" (2 Cor. 2:4, NKJV). Often the people who have wounded us most are the people we love. Bitterness is a stumbling block that prevents healing from taking place in both parties, but God's *agape* love opens the door for restoration to take place through forgiveness and godly, caring correction.

Paul chose to rebuke Peter publicly, but in most cases confrontation as a part of releasing bitterness is best done in the company of a trusted, proven Christian leader. Choose a non-threatening environment, if possible.

Finally, wherever you choose to have this confrontation, believe for a positive outcome. Pray before, during, and after the confrontation for the person you are approaching. You must be prepared to hear answers to questions that may further hurt you in some cases.

Confrontations are not a one-off. Sometimes this step will bring up new emotions and new issues to bring before the Lord. That is OK. Submit to this process and allow the Holy Spirit to show you how to deal with these new developments. This is essential to ensure your heart attitude is right and that the spirit of bitterness will have no open door to gain a foothold back in your life.

Even under the umbrella of these guidelines, there are several ways a person can attempt a confrontation. However, there are also wrong ways to approach conformation. Accusation and blame are two such ways. These approaches often do not end well for either party. If this abrasive approach is taken, this will, in no uncertain terms, provoke a negative response from the offender.

Also, you must keep in mind that unless a person becomes sorrowful for their actions, which would lead to repentance, salvation, and a radical change in behavior, it is likely nothing else will change in the life of the person you are confronting. That is OK; you are released from any further responsibility to that person. You must rest in knowing you did what you needed to do and then move on. The whole point of this step is to gain relief, so allow the experience to free you, and then release the person to God.

As you prepare for, engage in, and then process this confrontation, you can pray this prayer to stir up holy boldness and remain rooted in these crucial components of the process:

> *Dear Father God, I come to You seeking courage and holy boldness. Your Word says in Jeremiah 1:8, "'Do not be afraid of them [or their hostile faces], For I am with you [always] to protect you and deliver you,' says the LORD"* (AMP). *Help me as I go to the one who has injured me. Help me not to be double-minded, and help me to craft my words so that they do no harm. Allow me to go with Your love in my heart and Your strength on my face. Show me how to display meekness and extend Your godly love of forgiveness and allow You to be gloried in the process. Amen.*

LIVE LIFE FORWARD

Just as Naomi had to confront her bitterness and those she blamed for the circumstances that made her bitter, we must understand confrontation can be therapeutic. It opens the door to needed dialogue, which potentially starts the healing process. Addressing wounds properly requires two vantage points: a spiritual and a natural one. In the natural, if a wound is not addressed properly, infection is the result. Additionally, if a wound is not addressed spiritually, infection also takes place in the form of a root of bitterness. What we are unwilling to confront we will never get past or resolve. Confrontation is a part of life! Many choose not to confront things or people for two reasons, accountability and fear. We all are to be held accountable for our role in all unpleasant events, regardless of how small it might be. And we must understand the spirit of fear is a demonic spirit that comes to keep you from God's best for your life. It comes to imprison you mentally and emotionally, causing you to live and walk through life with a spirit of timidity.

Living life forward is a choice. Being stuck in bitterness and becoming a victim of the silent killer is a choice. If you want to embrace God's best, an introspective examination about fragile relationships, traumatic events, and how you see yourself must be done. Self-evaluation of the condition of our heart is essential if we are ever going to confront the spirit of bitterness and look the silent killer right in the eyes. No more hiding or avoiding this issue. Face it! Uncover and uproot all roots of bitterness. Any demonic growth and hatchlings that produce weeds choke out God's best for our lives.

Understand that on the other side confrontation is relief. Jesus stated in the Bible, "The thief does not come except to steal, and to kill, and to destroy. I have come that they may have life, and that may have it more abundantly" (John 10:10, NKJV). Jesus is stating the devil does not want any person to face their hurts. In fact, he is the person behind your pain. It could have been your mother, father, husband, relative, a foe, or a stranger that carried out the devilish deed, but you must know that they received orders from an ancient, demonic spirit to bring you harm. Choose to confront the demons of your pain. Release yourself from the memory of the injury and walk away from this self-imposed prison forever.

Chapter 10

EXTENDING GRACE

For the LORD God is a sun and shield: the LORD
will give grace and glory: no good thing will he
withhold from them that walk uprightly.
—PSALM 84:11

THERE ARE MANY things we can all benefit from that can help enrich our individual lives: money, love, and divine health, to name a few. However, we should all agree on one thing, and that is, God's favor is more profitable and valuable than any human commodity or resource. It is a divine endowment that you can't touch or feel, but you and others know it when a person has it on their lives. Grace gives a person a heavenly edge in life. The person who has favor covering their life is empowered like no other. An example of this empowerment can be seen in how they handle offenses when they have been abused. We have looked at all the reasons why it is important—necessary, even— for people to forgive their abusers. However, the person who has grace from God covering them will acknowledge that they have been offended, but then they choose to take the high road and cast all their cares, hurts, and pains on their heavenly Father. This allows the person to release the grace of God immediately out of their reservoir of divine love.

The Greek word for "grace" is *charis*. One dictionary tells us that *charis* means "that which affords joy, pleasure...loveliness." It refers to "good will, loving-kindness, and favour [sic]," specifically the "merciful kindness" of the Lord that brings people to Christ and "increases them in Christian faith."[1] *Grace* in the Hebrew is *chanan*, "to be gracious, show favor...to have mercy on."[2] In modern times we understand *grace* to mean "unmerited favor." The grace-filled person understands it's not enough just to forgive, but they also need to extend grace to their abuser and enemies.

Why is it not enough just to forgive the people who have injured you? With forgiveness, there are always lingering consequences because of the actions of the abuser. What is grace from God's perspective? Grace is forgiveness without consequences! Grace is God's unmerited favor! It's His charity toward man. It is a benevolent disposition, always giving a person better than he or she deserves. Simply put, it is heavenly favor, a divine gift, whereas forgiveness is the decision to exercise mercy over an incident only.

Grace, like forgiveness, does not find its origin with man. Grace originates with God and flows from God.

According to the Bible, grace comes from the abundance of love within God's heart: "But may the God of all grace, who called us to His eternal glory by Christ Jesus, after you have suffered a while, perfect, establish, strengthen, and settle you (1 Pet. 5:10, NKJV). Grace resets a person back to a place of purity and wholeness without fault-finding.

To understand God's grace better, try to understand the analogy of a good parent who gives a child some gifts at Christmastime. The parent does not look to see if the child has been naughty or nice. The child just receives the gifts from his or her loving parents. Grace is the same for the Christian. The Bible states that the Christian is extended salvation by grace: "For by grace you have been saved through faith; and that not of yourselves: it is the gift of God: Not of works, lest any man should boast" (Eph. 2:8–9, NKJV).

People who love God reverence His Word and are often receivers of a life laden with His grace and godly favor. Examples of such people can be found in the Bible. A shepherd boy named David was such a person. He was nobody by today's standards, a boy who lived on the other side of the tracks. He was the last son of an old man named Jesse, a sheep keeper. Because David loved God and cultivated a relationship with Him, he received grace and favor from God. He became king of Israel. Joseph was also the last son of his father, Jacob. Joseph was a son who loved God and lived a godly life, and God graced and favored his life. God's grace made everything Joseph did to prosper! God's grace and favor followed, protected, provided for, and exalted him. He became a very prominent, respected, and established person in due time. So, we see it is God Himself who initiates pardons of man's sinful life and extends His grace (favor) toward man, which allows him to accomplish great feats in his life.

Why would anyone want to extend grace to people who have injured them? Simple: to bring men to a mental and spiritual state of repentance. Just as God's grace also provides a means of reconciliation for man to reestablish his original relationship with God, extending that grace to others helps reconcile human relationships and reestablish them on a better, healthier foundation. How is this possible? The spirit of grace teaches the abusers to deny ungodliness and "live soberly, righteously," according to Titus 2:11–12 (NKJV). Once they receive His grace, enhancement comes to them. We must understand that "all have sinned and fallen short of the glory of God, being justified [found not guilty] freely by His grace through the redemption that is in Christ Jesus" (Rom. 3:23, NKJV). Grace wipes the slate clean!

When attempting to extend grace to people who abused, rejected, or slandered your name, you must first go to a specific place to receive godly instructions about God's grace. Grace is dispensed in abundance at this specific location. The dispensing station is none other than the throne of God, the throne of grace. The Bible directs the believer, "Let us therefore come boldly to the throne of grace, that we may obtain mercy and find grace to help in time of need" (Heb. 4:16, NKJV).

How do you extend grace to someone who has hurt you? We should follow Jesus's model of extending grace to understand it better. The Bible states that "God demonstrates His own love toward us, in that while we were still sinners, Christ died for us" (Rom. 5:8, NKJV). Christine Hoover, author of the article "What Does It Mean to Give Grace to One Another," takes it further by saying:

> In his grace toward us, God says, "I see your sin. I name your sin specifically to you through conviction of the Holy Spirit. I have made a way for your specific sin to be dealt with at the cross of Christ. You don't have to cover it or ignore it or try to deal with it on your own."[3]

Grace has a specific purpose in a person's life. It carries a breaker's anointing to release, empower, and teach people to overcome sin. (See Romans 5:20, NKJV.) It is help and support when needed, help for the immediate and present! There are many people in the world who receive help in their time of need, only to return to destructive patterns and cycles that move them out of the will of God for their lives. However, grace should have a transformative effect on people's heart and life.

You must understand there are limitations to divine

grace. Likewise, there is a responsibility in receiving the grace of God carelessly. The Bible sends a stern warning about receiving the grace in vain. The Word of God states, "We then, as workers together with Him, also plead with you not to receive the grace of God in vain" (2 Cor. 6:1, NKJV). Many people who receive the grace of God do not respect, nor value, the gift and do nothing but take it for granted and squander the grace of God.

God wants His followers to maximize His gift and grow in His grace. It is not a suggestion but a command from God: "But grow in the grace and knowledge of our Lord and Savior Jesus Christ. To Him be the glory both now and forever. Amen" (2 Pet. 3:18, NKJV). The Scriptures tell people to truly understand that growth is a part of our walk in grace. We first must learn to appreciate what Jesus Christ has already done for us. We should have a more intimate understanding of the sacrifice that was made on our behalf and the love that was extended toward mankind. This does not just mean grasping the sacrificial death, burial, and resurrection of Christ but the investment into people becoming more Christlike daily.

We must remember grace is an extension of God's love toward us. Oftentimes when a person attempts to extend grace it is on a merit system. But Christians are not to operate independently of God. The problem with man-made merit systems is that these people must constantly live up to a vacillating system and constantly prove themselves before grace is given. To prevent this from happening, we are told to consult God always. He will lead us and instruct us on how and what steps we should follow to release His grace properly. Following these precise instructions allows man to receive from God so that God can get the glory out of the situation, which will compel the bitter person to want to become Christlike.

BITTERNESS ACTS AS A ROADBLOCK TO GRACE

The teachings of the Bible admonish the believer to expect and welcome transformation of the mind and heart. When the mind is exposed to the teachings of God and the heart accepts and embraces these teachings, expansion comes to the mind. This expansion takes place like a pregnant woman who grows physically until eventually, at the right time, her child comes bursting out of her womb. So is it with extending grace! It is a process of internal growth versus something that can automatically be expressed externally.

Throughout the process and after, the silent killer of bitterness will do all it can to keep the offended person from ever moving into a place where he or she can be healed. This is accomplished by having the injured party constantly rehearse or relive the traumatic event. By constantly highlighting the negativity that surrounds the trauma, the wound remains raw, the emotions stay unsettled, and the bitter root in the person's soul is strengthened. This keeps them bound and stuck in their emotions. It will cause you to live a life of silent misery accompanied with private pain. That ever-present pain will continue to haunt you and make life miserable! If people harboring bitterness refuse to deal with the root of bitterness head on, they will never be able to come to a place in their heart where they can forgive and thus extend grace to the people who have injured them.

The silent killer of bitterness is also working overtime attempting to keep people ignorant of the Word of God, because the devil knows that revelation from the Word will set people free. The devil understands that if he can keep someone ignorant of God's Word, he can suggest to them that it is in their best interest to allow bitterness to get a solid hold on their heart. Unbeknownst to them, they become noncompliant to God's Word. Then they slowly begin to compromise and eventually leave the eternal truths of God's Word, which bring life and blessings. Once that happens, what avenue does a bitter person even drive on to get to a destination where they have access to genuine grace if they don't believe in the teaching of the Bible? What other teaching will they employ in the matter? These people often just self-medicate or use New Age methods of treatment or avoidance, like hypnosis, to access some counterfeit type of grace. The Bible states, "My people are destroyed for lack of knowledge" (Hosea 4:6). Knowledge of God's Word and applying His eternal truth are the secrets to true success in life. His Word teaches us how to handle every situation that believers may be confronted with.

The devil understands quite well the result of this compromised mind-set and ignorance of the Word! He allowed himself to become consumed with pride and arrogance. This was his downfall. He also poisoned the hearts and minds of one-third of the angels in heaven. Therefore, the Bible states this of his fate: "Yet you shall be brought down to Sheol [Hell], to the lowest depths of the Pit" (Isa. 14:14, NKJV). The Bible goes on to say he was thrown out of heaven.

> And war broke out in heaven: Michael and his angels fought with the dragon; and the dragon and his angels fought, but they did not prevail, nor was a place found for them in heaven any longer. So the great dragon was cast out, that serpent of old, called the Devil and Satan, who deceives the whole world; he was cast to the earth, and his angels were cast out with him.
>
> —REVELATION 12:7–9, NKJV

The devil and the rebellious, non-compliant angels were cast to Earth. Demonic bitterness set into Lucifer's heart because he was thrown out of heaven. Lucifer was one of three archangels mentioned in Scripture. He was created by God, just as all angles were. His name means "day star" or "son of the morning." Instead of living up to his name, he chose to bring darkness and shroud himself in confusion.

Satan is shrewd. He understands that if he can deceive us into harboring bitterness toward anyone he can cause us to fall from grace ourselves. The Scriptures say we are to look "carefully least anyone fall short of the grace of God; lest any root of bitterness springing up cause trouble, and by this many become defiled" (Heb. 12:15, NKJV). Author Dale A. Robbins says, "The scriptures make it very clear that the person who withholds forgiveness [grace] is not right with God."[4] The apostle Paul had this to say about the dangers of harboring bitterness: "And do not grieve the Holy Spirit of God, by whom you were sealed for the day of redemption. Let all bitterness, wrath, anger, clamor, and evil speaking be put away from you, with all malice. And be kind to one another, tenderhearted, forgiving one another, even as God in Christ forgave you" (Eph. 4:30–32, NKJV). Love is the key! A heart void of brotherly love (*phileo* in Greek) is unable to forgive, let alone extend grace.

LONGSUFFERING GRACE

If we have carefully read the previous chapters we can conclude that there is tremendous value in having a godly character and lifestyle. The benchmark characteristics of this lifestyle can be found in the fruit of the Spirit:

> But the fruit of the Spirit is love, joy, peace, long-suffering, gentleness, goodness, faith, meekness, temperance.
>
> —GALATIANS 5:22–23

The grace we extend to others finds itself buried in the definition of longsuffering. The Greek word for "longsuffering" is *makrothumia*, which means "patient endurance; to bear long with the frailties, offenses, injuries, and provocations of others, without murmuring, repining, or resentment."[5] It is here, by extending God's divine love, where grace is birth out and delivered to the bitter world, specifically to the person or people who have injured or wounded you. God's grace—an expression of divine love—is the antidote for the root of bitterness! His love, which is also deputized with heavenly authority, casts out the spirit of bitterness with its foul and nauseating stench. God's grace finally captures and imprisons this hateful, wicked, and repugnant spirit known as the silent killer forever.

Chapter 11

GOD'S LOVE COVERS

*Most importantly, love each other deeply [ear-
nestly], because love will cause people to forgive each
other for many sins [covers a multitude of sins.*
—1 PETER 4:8, EXV

T HE WORD *LOVE* has many different meanings to
people in today's world. A word that was origi-
nally meant to show extreme feelings of endear-
ment often is used so casually that it seems to dilute
or weaken the true intent of the word. The English language seems to be growing by the day with words that
would describe and give life and meaning to so many
things. Today there are new dictionaries that have been
created to house such words. However, within every dictionary you will find the word *love*—a word that every
human being wants to have personified and visible in
their life.

There are various definitions for *love*. Merriam-
Webster defines *love* as "a feeling of strong or constant
affection for a person." It is "attraction that includes

sexual desire: the strong affection felt by people who have a romantic relationship; a person you love in a romantic way."[1] It appears these definitions have a strong sense of sensual love. It appears that the English definition of *love* is very limited, and it tries to squeeze several meanings into the same word. Therefore, let us look at the Greek definitions for *love,* since the Greek language offers a wider and more exhaustive meaning for the word.

It appears that Greek is a bit more sophisticated than English. In English we have one word, *love,* for the different types of affection and relationships that the Greek language takes six words to describe. That's right; in Greek, there are six different words for "love."[2] For our purposes, we will only look at three of these words and their definitions.

1. Eros, or sexual passion

Eros refers to the love of the body. According to Roman Krznaric, author of an article titled "The Ancient Greeks' 6 Words for Love (And Why Knowing Them Can Change Your Life)":

> This first kind of love...[is] named after the Greek god of fertility, and it represented the idea of sexual passion and desire....[It] was viewed as dangerous, fiery, and irrational form of love that could take hold of you and possess you—an attitude shared by many later spiritual thinkers, such as the Christian writer C.S. Lewis."[3]

2. Phileo, or deep friendship

Phileo refers to "love of the soul."[4] Again, Krznaric writes, "Philea [sic] concerned the deep comradely friendship that developed between brothers in arms who had fought side by side in the battlefield. It was about showing loyalty to your friends, sacrificing for them."[5]

3. Agape

Agape is "selfless love."[6] It is unconditional love that sees beyond the outer surface and accepts a person for who he/she is. It is "a sacrificial kind of love."[7] In his book *The Four Loves,* "C. S. Lewis referred to it as 'gift love,' the highest form of Christian love."[8]

Since forgiveness is rooted in love, this in-depth look at the different types of love allows us to gain a more complete picture of where forgiveness comes from.

IT'S TIME TO EVALUATE

Many other religions or practices espouse the idea that to truly eliminate bitterness out of a person's life there first must be a deliverer available to the embittered person. Many religions point to a god or gods who can serve this purpose. There have also been historical leaders seen as deliverers that have used various methods to fight injustices, financial, and racial inequalities, along with fighting the spirit of hate. World figures like Mahatma Gandhi, Martin Luther King Jr., and Nelson Mandela are all seen as deliverers because they were leaders who had some measure of success in their fight to improve the inequities of life. Nonetheless, all these gods, all these human figures, were and are all limited in power and influence. Jesus Christ is the one true Deliverer, and there has never been anyone like Him.

One of main differences between Jesus Christ and the human deliverers is He is not just a world figure but the Son of God Himself. He has all power and universal influence at His fingertips. He was sent as a gift to all humanity to release them from the trappings of the world and demonic bondages. If there is one central theme that personified Jesus life and ministry it was that of genuine *agape* love. This is all part of the promise of John 3:16: "God so loved the world that He gave His only begotten Son, that whoever believes in Him should not perish but have everlasting life" (NKJV). This *agape* love, extended to us, is transformative in nature and unlike anything else the world can offer.

Throughout the process of gaining freedom from the spirit of bitterness we have discussed over and over again that the love of God must be our foundation. It is step one in the process of evicting the silent killer, but reinforcing that foundation and ensuring you are operating in love so that the spirit of bitterness has no room to operate is a crucial part of each subsequent step as well. Now—after you have confronted the one(s) who hurt you and before you continue—is the time to stop and seriously reassess the condition of your heart, memories, and the role of love in your actions and behavior.

Jesus understood genuine love covers a multitude of offenses and sins (1 Pet. 4:8, NKJV). It is this love that will also cover any lingering memories and fill your heart so that there is no room for bitterness to remain. Many bitter people subconsciously file memories and details of what happened to them away for safe keeping in their minds. They keep detailed mental records of each incident and everyone who was involved in their mind. Once you have forgiven those who hurt you and have confronted them, it is time to look inward and see if any of these memories remain. If they do, expose them, turn them over to the Lord, and ask Him to cover them with His love and deliver you from those memories so that you can be free of them forever.

There are certain people who have been victimized and have sustained horrendous attacks verbally, emotionally, and physically against their person. These people have been injured so deeply that they have been left with emotional and physical wounds that they have lived with for years. These people live in a self-imposed prison long after they sustain the attack. Many choose to try and free themselves by anesthetizing their pain in variety of ways, from becoming chemically dependent to seeking secular counseling, over-eating, succumbing to depression, and last, by harboring bitterness. These behaviors, like the bitter roots that produced them, can take time to overcome, even with the help of the Holy

Spirit. In some cases confronting the person or people who hurt them can bring up new memories or create fresh wounds. That's why the person who has harbored roots of bitterness within their heart truly should stop at this point and ask himself or herself the question, Why did I hold on to painful memories of my past and strengthen my bitterness? While examining their heart the once-embittered person should look for evidence of both lingering bitterness and genuine love within them. Whether they find bitterness or love, the next act is the same: ask, Do I want to be free? If the answer is yes, keep moving forward. Refuse to hold on to bitterness and pursue the peace of God.

Love Is the Key to Ongoing Freedom

Many people go to extreme lengths to try to display romantic love. Many spend millions of dollars annually on material possessions and gifts, all given to show they love someone. In spite of all our human effort toward demonstrating *eros* love, is this truly the kind of love that matters most? Not by a long shot.

So why is the love of Christ not displayed more in the world today? People withhold this transformative, healing love because of an intentional decision not to release people from the grudges they are holding against them. Author Richard Savage writes, "It is impossible to love somebody and at the same time hold the bad things they may have done in the past against them."[9] Unfortunately, the world we live in today is a world where people want to see the person(s) who hurt them suffer by any means—legal, illegal, vigilantism, sickness, or even bad luck. Savage goes on to say:

> More commonly, people keep a record of one anothers' [sic] wrongs because their pride has been offended, or their property damaged, and they want revenge or to see the other person humiliated in some way, even when what happened was done in ignorance or accidentally. This is far away from God's love and the excitement and joy there is in heaven when a sinner repents and never wants to sin again. Jesus could say on the cross: "Father, forgive them, for they do not know what they do" (Luke 23:34).[10]

The enemy of our soul, Satan, has a vested interest in helping and encouraging people who have been wounded unfairly or who had a life of bad breaks to hold grudges. This type of mind-set fosters an independent spirit, a spirit of unforgiveness, promotes revenge, and fosters bitterness, leaving no room or authority for God to bring resolution and healing to both the offended party and the abuser. You cannot stay free of the silent killer as long as you give in to this mind-set and withhold love from those around you, regardless of what they have done. Our world is so blinded by Satan's tactic that it is ignorant of this command from God: "My friends, do not try to punish others when they wrong you [take revenge, avenge yourselves], but wait for God to punish them with his anger [leave room for [God's] wrath]. It is written: 'I will punish those who do wrong [vengeance is mine]; I will repay them'" (Deut. 32:35, NCV). If you want to uproot the spirit of bitterness from your life for good, you must heed this scripture and continually turn those who offend you over to the Lord for His judgment.

The enemy of your soul will try to make God and His judgments look bad. As we discussed in chapter 7, he does this by highlighting negative events in our lives and suggesting that God allowed and could have diverted them but did not. He also does it with subtle whispers that suggest God's punishments are not as good as our human revenge. God understands we are human and therefore weak and tend to try to filter life's unpleasant moments through our humanity instead of our renewed spirit. Christ knows firsthand what it is like to be tempted by the voice of the enemy. That's why He tells His followers, "So I tell you: Live [Walk] by following [guided by; in the power of; by] the Spirit. Then you will not do what your sinful self [sinful nature; flesh] wants [desires; craves]" (Gal. 5:16, EXV). The devil would have you to believe that God does not keep His Word, nor does He really care about man and his problems, but this is a lie. God reminds his followers, "I will never leave you nor forsake you" (Heb. 13:5, NKJV). God ensures His followers He will be loyal to them regardless of the situation. It is our job to have faith in Him and in His sovereignty and trust that He will work all things out perfectly. When you feel the enemy whispering in your ear, remind yourself of Hebrews 6:18: "It is impossible for God to lie" (NKJV). Therefore, if He made you a promise, you can take him at His word.

God implores His followers to "let him have all [their] worries and cares, for he is always thinking about you and watching everything that concerns you" (1 Pet. 5:7, TLB). As soon as you are offended, immediately turn to the Lord and hand your pain to Him. Refuse to entertain the suggestions of the enemy. Ask God for discernment, and make love your reflex instead of offense. If you try to navigate your feelings and heal your wounded emotions yourself, you will only delay the healing process and cause your pain to remain present longer. You will risk falling prey once again to the spirit of bitterness.

Love Was the Key to Naomi's Freedom

Earlier in this book we spent a good deal of time talking about the events that caused Naomi to harbor the spirit of bitterness. Now we will examine her path to freedom. Naomi's journey to wholeness may or may not have followed the steps we have discussed in this book; the Scriptures don't give us enough detail to determine if she acknowledged the spiritual nature of her bitterness and turned to the Lord, forgave herself and others, confronted the source of her pain, and then consciously extended grace. We do know that at some point in the process she made the decision to selflessly love her daughter-in-law Ruth in the midst of her bitterness, and that conscious demonstration of *agape* love transformed their lives and paved the way for the birth of Christ generations later.

Let's start with a recap of what we know: Naomi, the wife of Elimelech, was a person who was full of bitterness. As we have seen, she was voiceless in her marriage and became a widow and single mother in one swoop, all in a male-dominated society and while alienated from the community in which she was raised. She eventually became childless, with seemingly no hope for a prosperous future. But Naomi was a follower of God, even though she was estranged from Bethlehem, and as we have seen, God is omniscient and "watching everything that concerns" us (1 Pet. 5:7, TLB). He was fully aware of the calamity and crisis that had hit Naomi life. He also understood that Naomi and her husband had made temporary decisions that had long-term ramifications for their family's life, and He had a plan for redeeming her life from the destructive path down which it seemed headed.

You see, God is a proactive God! When Adam sinned in the garden and fell from grace because of the influence and suggestions of the serpent, God, being omniscient, already had a restoration plan in place for man. Like His plan for Naomi's life, He intended to unveil it at a strategic time through a sacrifice that would serve as payment to satisfy God's penalty for mankind's rebellion. Jesus's death on the cross would serve as the catalyst for releasing God's love to the world once again.

The Scriptures state that God is a good God, and He provides for his children. Often God is good to us, even when we are not good to him. Many abandon His percepts and Word, only to find God is constantly faithful and reliable. Even far down the path they chose— a path that took them away from God's will for their life, they discover that they have a dependable and reliable God who is also a restorer. As God sent Jesus to be the Restorer for God, He is also able to restore the person who has sustained loss and is harboring bitterness. Many times, people tend to think God is oblivious to their pain and plight, but on the contrary He is using what was meant to destroy you to reposition you closer to Himself and allow you to see a different vantage point about the great love He has toward a mankind. This is exactly what Naomi discovered when she returned to Bethlehem.

Regardless of how the women who had gathered to witness Naomi's return viewed her current plight, regardless of what Naomi was spewing out of her mouth, and regardless of her displaced anger, God was yet in control of her life and circumstances. His *agape* love for her ignited the embers of love that remained buried, almost burnt out, within her heart. Naomi had a choice to continue to feel sorry for herself or to step away from her bitterness in order to focus on the task of helping her daughter-in-law, the other widow, Ruth. By becoming a mentor and guide to this newfound follower of God, Naomi became consumed with the task of guiding this young woman to find redemption. In the process, she experienced a life-saving encounter with her own Redeemer and finally eradicated the root of bitterness from her life.

Through the process of events, Boaz, a distant, wealthy relative of Naomi, redeemed Ruth and made her his wife. Now, it is worth clarifying that he was wealthy, but this relationship was based in Israelite tradition; this is not a sugar daddy situation in any way. Boaz—whose name means "mighty man of valor" or "a man of position and wealth"—redeemed Ruth (and therefore Naomi) by "buying them back" from the life for which they were destined in a legal transaction that involved the elders of the city. Boaz was taking the necessary steps to legitimize Ruth and Naomi, thus walking in the role of a redeemer. This role was further clarified when Ruth became pregnant and bore a son to Boaz, which ensured Ruth and Naomi would always have family to provide for them and which restored Naomi's lineage. By acting as their redeemer, Boaz became a type (foreshadowing) of Christ.

The same women of the town who greeted Naomi and barely recognized her because of her changed appearance began to sing praises to God for the love He extended toward Naomi.

> Then the women said to Naomi, "Blessed be the Lord, who has not left you this day without a close relative; and may his name be famous in

Israel! And may he be to you a restorer of life and a nourisher of your old age; for your daughter-in-law, who loves you, who is better to you than seven sons, has borne him." Then Naomi took the child and laid him on her bosom, and became a nurse to him.

—Ruth 4:14–17, NKJV

God, from His lofty position, is still able to be in touch with our infirmities and weaknesses. He daily extends His grace and favor and love toward our lives. As God redeemed Naomi's life from bitterness and potential destruction, He stands ready to maneuver in our daily lives to retrieve and reposition the parts of our heart that have been ravished by the silent killer of bitterness.

Just as Naomi's action in response to God's love changed the course of her life, people must choose to accept His invitation as He draws us to His loving kindness. There's not enough room within your heart for bitterness and God. We must choose to allow His Spirit to fill our heart with His love so that no bitterness, unforgiveness, or memory of the offenses of others against us, remains. He restored Naomi's life this way, and He stands at the door and knocks at your heart. His desires to help you become whole again and finally uproot the spirit of bitterness for good. Will you allow Him this total access to your heart? You determine what goes and who remains. Choose well!

Chapter 12

FROM BITTER TO SWEET:
A HEART SET FREE

The horse is prepared for the day of battle, but deliverance is of the LORD.
—PROVERBS 21:31, NKJV

THE PEOPLE WHO are fortunate enough to have valuable jewelry, treasury notes, stock certificates, annuities, large sums of cash money, and other types of valuables assets are people who usually go to extremes to secure their valuable assets. They do their best to keep them under lock and key because these items hold great value to them. It should be the same when it come to a person's heart that has been delivered from demonic bondage. The value of material assets fluctuates; therefore, their true value is never really assured. However, you cannot attach a price tag to the transformed mind or renewed spirit of a person who has been delivered from any type of chemical dependency, from identity issues, or from the spirit of bitterness, to name only a few types of bondage. In these instances it is how one values his or her deliverance that matters. The Scriptures state, "For where your treasure is, there your heart will be also" (Matt. 6:21, NKJV).

To get a truly clear picture of this I will use the scenario of a person wrongly accused of a crime as an example. When new evidence proves a person innocent and then that person is released from the captivity, the joy and freedom felt by that newly freed person is indescribable. The person is now able to move around without restraints again, along with having his or her life returned to a state of normalcy. This change produces a feeling of euphoria for that person. The value of their freedom from bondage is enormous.

Being bound in any way is a horrible feeling, and being released from that bondage—be it spiritual, physical, mental, or emotional—is liberating. I can attest to this as a person who was previously bound. Nevertheless, any newly freed person must understand that there is a responsibility that comes with freedom. If an inmate who has been released from prison is going to remain free, he must rid himself of any destructive behavior and separate himself from people who could potentially cause him to have a relapse. This also applies to spiritual matters as well. To walk (live) in a place of wholeness and maintain a life that is pleasing to God, the person who has experienced deliverance must choose to maintain a heart of deliverance with understanding.

With respect to the spirit of bitterness, this means

the offended party must no longer be willing to allow the spirit of bitterness to have free reign in their lives. You will find yourself falling back into the clutches of bitterness if you forget that the silent killer will terrorize you as soon as you deny or neglect to consider that it poses a genuine threat to your peace and health. This means making a choice to have a predetermined mind-set that says, "I will not react to any negative situations in my life in a worldly or anti-God manner. Instead, I will make an agreement within myself that says I will respond to negativity with love instead of merely reacting." Responding allows a person a moment of clarity to gather their thoughts and determine what is the most productive way of dealing with the situation. If he or she has the mind-set to keep peace, the offended party will have success in trying to forgive the person or people who have hurt them.

Remember that we all must be knowledgeable of the fact that trouble sometimes comes looking for you. A person does not necessarily have to be living an unruly life to be involved in some type of calamity or misfortune. Job stated, "Man who is born of a woman is of few days and full of trouble" (Job 14:1, NKJV).

If one were to read the account of the life of Job within the Bible you would find this man was living a very prosperous life. He was a land owner and a respected man in the community. He was a business man, a father, a husband, a son, a mentor, and a wealthy man. He was "blameless and upright, and one who feared God and shunned evil" (Job 1:1, NKJV). Yet, trouble still found him and tried to turn Job's heart toward bitterness so that he would blame God. After Job was delivered and restored from his calamity of pain and suffering, he had to learn to be thankful and also alert for surprise demonic terrorist attacks.

First Peter 5:8 issues us this warning: "Be sober, be vigilant; because your adversary the devil walks about like a roaring lion, seeking whom he may devour" (NKJV). Any time you are attempting to live a righteous life you become a target for the enemy of your soul, the devil. He hates any person who is attempting to live by biblical standards and percepts. He sees this type of person as a threat to his kingdom; therefore, he has extreme animosity for anyone who chooses to become a follower of God and embrace and practice Christianity as a lifestyle.

We must be ever ready to do battle against certain attack from the enemy. Proverbs 21:31 says, "The horse is prepared for the day of battle, But deliverance is of the LORD" (NKJV). The scripture above gives an accurate picture of a war horse that is prepared for battle. The horse will not shy away from oncoming danger, nor will he become spooked from loud shouts or explosions from the enemy. The horse has a resolve to serve and fight to the death. The horse takes this approach because he is confident in his master, the rider. So, it should be with Christians. Any person who chooses to accept the invitation from God should have ultimate confidence in

God, His abilities, and the promises that He spells out in His Word.

The Christian must also understand three important things. First, the kingdom of God is the most powerful entity in the universe. Second, the kingdom has no lack of any kind. Finally, understand the enemies of God are constantly trying to attack the kingdom and bring it to ruin. So, when entering the kingdom of God, know you are entering a kingdom that is involved in an intergalactic cosmic conflict with the forces of darkness.

With this understanding and to ensure continuous victories in every area of life, the Christian is told to be careful how he clothes himself. The Christian is told to "put on the whole armor of God, that you may be able to stand against the wiles of the devil" (Eph. 6:11, NKJV). This spiritual armor protects the individual from attacks from the devil. The person that has gone through deliverance and in whom the bitter root has been exposed, excavated, and eradicated from their heart must choose to live with new spiritual armor to ensure his safety and to protect him from being infected with the spirit of bitterness once again. If a person has chosen to use alternative strategies (outside of biblical strategies) to maintain a pure heart, the question should be asked, What is the recidivism rate with people using these alternative techniques?

If you once harbored the silent killer of bitterness and are now free because of what God has done for you, you should want to follow a stringent path to remain free from any type of bondage. It is critical that you keep it at the forefront of your mind that bitterness is an ancient, demonic spirit! The Scriptures send repeated warnings to you, the delivered person, to arm yourself with spiritual weapons and expect the demonic spirit to try and infiltrate your emotions and attitude once again. Jesus Himself issued one of the strongest such warnings:

> When an unclean spirit goes out of a man, he goes through dry places, seeking rest, and finds none. Then he says, "I will return to my house from which I came." And when he comes, he finds it empty, swept, and put in order. Then he goes and takes with him seven other spirits more wicked than himself, and they enter and dwell there; and the last state of that man is worse than the first. So shall it also be with this wicked generation.
> —MATTHEW 12:43–45, NKJV

Deliverance is costly. Therefore, guard your heart and remain alert. Acknowledge God when you are tempted to respond in a negative manner and refuse to listen to the whisperings of the enemy. Stay rooted in love, and give the spirit of bitterness no ground to take in your heart.

Maintaining your deliverance requires a deliberate choice not to be bound ever again. You must understand that bitterness is always there crouching at the door like a lion ready to pounce on you and devour you.

Do not forget that bitterness is the result of a heart that refuses to forgive. How often should anyone forgive a person? What are the limitations and boundaries on forgiveness? Remember, Jesus told Peter to forgive "up to seventy times seven" times (Matt. 18:22, NKJV). As we discussed previously, this number is representative of the command to forgive without limitation. Jesus was simply trying to say to have a mind-set to continuously forgive the abuser.

Regardless of what the world says, forgiving someone does not show you are a weak person but that you are strong! We live in a fallen, anti-God world that has different morals and values than the kingdom of God does. If you are going to live in this world, you must understand at some point in your life you will be injured by someone; however, you determine if you will allow the offense, no matter how egregious, to cause you to sin and become bitter. Put on the armor of God, prepare yourself for battle at any moment, and refuse to let down the guard of your heart. Choose love and forgiveness. Choose not to harbor the silent killer of bitterness, and choose to live your life offense free in the liberty Christ bought for you with His own blood! As a newly freed individual, you must know it was never God's plan that you be hurt or enslaved by bitterness. God said, "'For I know the plans and thoughts that I have for you,' says the LORD, 'plans for peace and well-being and not for disaster, to give you a future and a hope'" (Jer. 29:11, AMP). This is His word for you today:

Now that you have cast your cares, hurts, and pain onto Me, be at peace! Envision walking into the newness of what I have planned for you, a life of liberty without demonic restraints, where you are the head and not the tail, where you are seated alongside of Me. It is a life of holistic wholeness, a life where you're seated high above all of the cares of earthly living and above all the demonic realms.

I invite you to dwell in the secret place in My presence, where I dwell! There you will learn to embrace the mind of Christ, experience the love of Christ, and know you are protected from the demonic arrows when you live with the full armor of God on.

Be assured that you are accepted in the beloved family of God with all its rights and privileges as a child of God. I give you authority once more. I give you the keys of the kingdom of heaven. "Whatever you bind on earth will be bound in heaven, and whatever you loose on earth will be loosed in heaven," according to Matthew 16:19 (NIV).

Expect sudden breakthrough blessings to be released into your life. Expect to have favor with God and man because you chose to trust Me and walk in righteousness.

The bitter root has been eradicated out of your heart. Now be filled once again with a fresh infilling of the Holy Spirit until your heart overflows. Always remember your heavenly Father is a no-limits God who has limitless plans for your life. Now live your life forward.

Appendix

BIBLICAL TRUTHS ON THE SPIRIT OF BITTERNESS[1]

ATTHEW 12:34 TELLS us, "Out of the abundance of the heart the mouth speaketh." If your heart is full of bitterness, your thoughts and speech will be full of bitterness; but if you fill your heart with the Scriptures, your mouth will speak words of life and not death. The Word of God has a lot to say about bitterness and the danger it poses to the heart, mind, and body. Here are some scriptures to feed your spirit, encourage your soul, and embolden you in your battle against the silent killer.

Kinds of bitterness

- The soul: "Wherefore is light given to him that is in misery, and life unto the bitter in soul" (Job 3:20).

- The heart: "The heart knoweth his own bitterness; and a stranger doth not intermeddle with his joy" (Prov. 14:10).

Causes of bitterness

We have discussed in great depth in this book the ways in which people's actions or behaviors can leave people wounded and lead to bitterness, but the Bible gives us insight into many other potential sources of bitterness.

- Words: "Who whet their tongue like a sword, and bend their bows to shoot their arrows, even bitter words" (Ps. 64:3).

- Death: "Then said Samuel, Bring ye hither to me Agag the king of the Amalekites. And Agag came unto him delicately. And Agag said, Surely the bitterness of death is past" (1 Sam. 15:32); "A voice was heard in Ramah, lamentation, and bitter weeping; Rahel weeping for her children refused to be comforted for her children, because they were not" (Jer. 31:15).

- Childlessness: "And [Elkanah] had two wives; the name of the one was Hannah, and the name of the other Peninnah: and Peninnah had children, but Hannah had no children...And [Hannah] was in bitterness of soul, and prayed unto the LORD, and wept sore" (1 Sam. 1:2, 10).

- A foolish son: "A foolish son is a grief to his father, and bitterness to her that bare him" (Prov. 17:25).

- A demanding woman: "And I find more bitter than death the woman, whose heart is snares and nets, and her hands as bands: whoso pleaseth God shall escape from her; but the sinner shall be taken by her" (Eccles. 7:26).

- Sin: "And I find more bitter than death the woman, whose heart is snares and nets, and her hands as bands: whoso pleaseth God shall escape from her; but the sinner shall be taken by her" (Eccl. 7:26).

- Death: "A voice was heard in Ramah, lamentation, and bitter weeping; Rahel weeping for her children refused to be comforted for her children, because they were not" (Jer. 31:15).

- Apostasy: See Acts 8:18–23.

Warnings against bitterness

A brother offended is harder to be won than a strong city: and their contentions are like the bars of a castle.

—PROVERBS 18:19

Husbands, love your wives, and be not bitter against them.

—COLOSSIANS 3:19

Looking diligently lest any man fail of the grace of God; lest any root of bitterness springing up trouble you, and thereby many be defiled.

—HEBREWS 12:15

If ye have bitter envying and strife in your hearts, glory not, and lie not against the truth.

—JAMES 3:14

Exhortation to forgive

Thou shalt not avenge, nor bear any grudge against the children of thy people, but thou shalt love thy neighbor as thyself: I am the LORD.

—LEVITICUS 19:18

He that covereth a transgression seeketh love; but he that repeateth a matter separateth very friends.

—PROVERBS 17:9

For if ye forgive men their trespasses, your heavenly Father will also forgive you: But if ye forgive not men their trespasses, neither will your Father forgive your trespasses.

—MATTHEW 6:14–15

And his lord was wroth, and delivered him to the tormentors, till he should pay all that was due unto him. So likewise shall My Heavenly Father do also unto you, if ye from your hearts forgive not everyone his brother their trespasses.

—MATTHEW 18:34–35

Let all bitterness, and wrath, and anger, and clamour, and evil speaking, be put away from you, with all malice: And be ye kind one to another, tenderhearted, forgiving one another, even as God for Christ's sake hath forgiven you.

—EPHESIANS 4:31–32

And above all things have fervent charity [love] among yourselves: for charity shall cover the multitude of sins.

—1 PETER 4:8

Therefore if thou bring thy gift to the altar, and there remembers that thy brother hath ought against thee; Leave there thy gift before the altar, and go thy way; first be reconciled to thy brother, and then come and offer thy gift.

—MATTHEW 5:23–24

And when ye stand praying, forgive, if ye have ought against any: that your Father also which is in heaven may forgive you your trespasses.

—MARK 11:25

Let not the sun go down upon your wrath: Neither give place to the devil.

—EPHESIANS 4:26–27

Brethren, I count not myself to have apprehended: but this one thing I do, forgetting those things which are behind [in the past], and reaching forth unto those things which are before.

—PHILIPPIANS 3:13

Forbearing one another, and forgiving one another, if any man have a quarrel against any: even as Christ forgave you, so also do ye.

—COLOSSIANS 3:13

God's promises for the bitter heart

We know that all things work together for good to them that love God, to them who are the called according to his purpose.

—ROMANS 8:28

Behold, for peace I had great bitterness: but thou hast in love to my soul delivered it from the pit of corruption: for thou hast cast all my sins behind thy back.

—ISAIAH 38:17

NOTES

INTRODUCTION

1. Lee Strobel, *God's Outrageous Claims* (Grand Rapids, MI: Zondervan, 2009)

CHAPTER 1: NAOMI'S STORY

1. See the New King James Version commentary on Ruth 1:2.
2. Bruce Routledge, "Moab," *BibleOdyssey.org*, accessed July 24, 2017, https://www.bibleodyssey.org/places/main-articles/moab.

CHAPTER 2: YOU'VE GOT A RIGHT TO BE MAD

1. *Merriam-Webster Online Dictionary*, Merriam-Webster, 2015, s.v. "friendly fire."
2. James Meeks, "Iraq war logs: How friendly fire from US troops became routine," *The Guardian*, October 22, 2010, accessed July 3, 2017, https://www.theguardian.com/world/2010/oct/22/american-troops-friendly-fire-iraq.
3. "Life Principle 6: The Principle of Sowing and Reaping," *InTouch Ministries*, July 6, 2014, accessed July 3, 2017, https://www.intouch.org/read/life-principle-6-the-principle-of-sowing-and-reaping.

CHAPTER 4: A CONVERSATION ABOUT BITTERNESS

1. Paula White, *Deal With It!* (Nashville, TN: Thomas Nelson, Inc., 2006).
2. George Simon, "Confronting the High Cost of Bitterness," *Counselling Resource*, September 19, 2011, accessed July 1, 2017, http://counsellingresource.com/features/2011/09/19/high-cost-bitterness/.
3. *Merriam-Webster Online Dictionary*, Merriam-Webster, 2015, s.v. "bitter."
4. Joselyn A. Hasty, *Fundamentally Flawed* (Sarasota, FL: First Edition Design Publishing, Inc., 2011).
5. Ibid.

CHAPTER 5: IT'S TIME TO DEAL WITH THE SILENT KILLER

1. Anneli Rufus, "Arrested Development," *Psychology Today*, December 18, 2008, accessed July 1, 2017, https://www.psychologytoday.com/blog/stuck/200812/arrested-development.

CHAPTER 6: APPREHENDING THE SILENT KILLER

1. Julia Layton, "How does the FBI decide who makes the Most Wanted list?" *How Stuff Works: Culture*, accessed July 2, 2017, http://people.howstuffworks.com/fbi-most-wanted.htm.
2. Ibid.
3. Elaine Walton, "The Role of Forgiveness in Healing Intimate Wounds: A Model for LDS Psychotherapists," *Issues in Religion and Psychotherapy* 23, no. 1 (1998): Article 7, accessed July 26, 2017, http://scholarsarchive.byu.edu/cgi/viewcontent.cgi?article=1389&context=irp.

CHAPTER 7: GETTING TO THE BITTER ROOT

1. "The Plant Root System Distinguishes from the Shoot, Its Functions," *Cropsreview.com*, accessed July 4, 2017, http://www.cropsreview.com/plant-root-system.html.
2. *Strong's Exhaustive Concordance, Hebrew,* accessed July 4, 2017, at *Bible Hub,* http://biblehub.com/hebrew/3820.htm, s.v. "3820, leb."
3. Walter A. Elwell and Philip W. Comfort, eds., *Tyndale Bible Dictionary* (Wheaton, IL: Tyndale House Publishers, Inc., 2001), s.v., "heart."
4. Ibid.
5. Susan Thomas, "Getting to the Root of Our Problems," *Bible Study Tools*, accessed July 5, 2017, http://www.biblestudytools.com/blogs/association-of-biblical-counselors/getting-to-the-root.html.
6. J. Preston Eby, "Just What Do You Mean Man Is a Free Moral Agent," *Tentmaker*, accessed July 1, 2017, http://www.tentmaker.org/articles/savior-of-the-world/FreeMoralAgent-Eby.html.
7. Wayne Jackson, "Does Free Agency Nullify Personal Responsibility?" *Christian Courier*, accessed July 1, 2017,

https://www.christiancourier.com/articles/839-does-free-agency-nullify-personal-responsibility.
8. Ibid.
9. *English Oxford Living Dictionaries,* Oxford University Press, 2017, s.v. "persecution."

CHAPTER 8: FORGIVE

1. Elwell and Comfort, eds., *Tyndale Bible Dictionary*, s.v. "forgiveness."
2. "Forgiveness Defined," *Greater Good Magazine* Online, accessed July 5, 2017, https://greatergood.berkeley.edu/forgiveness/definition.
3. Robert Muller, quoted at *Think Exist*, accessed July 5, 2017, http://thinkexist.com/quotation/to-forgive-is-the-highest-most-beautiful-form-of/390790.html.
4. John Eckhardt, *Destroying the Spirit of Rejection* (Lake Mary, FL: Charisma House, 2016).
5. "Life Principle 6: The Principle of Sowing and Reaping," accessed July 3, 2017, https://www.intouch.org/read/life-principle-6-the-principle-of-sowing-and-reaping.

CHAPTER 9: CONFRONTED

1. "Avoidance—A Christian Problem," *Patheos*, September 21, 2011, accessed July 27, 2017, http://www.patheos.com/blogs/bibleandculture/2011/09/21/avoidance-a-christian-problem/.
2. Deborah Smith Pegues, *Confronting Without Offending* (Eugene, OR: Harvest House Publishers, 2009).

CHAPTER 10: EXTENDING GRACE

1. "The NAS New Testament Greek Lexicon," *Bible Study Tools*, s.v., "charis," accessed July 7, 2017, http://www.biblestudytools.com/lexicons/greek/nas/charis.html. *Charis* is Strong's number 5485.
2. "The KJV Old Testament Hebrew Lexicon," *Bible Study Tools*, s.v., "chanan," accessed July 7, 2017, http://www.biblestudytools.com/lexicons/hebrew/kjv/chanan.html. *Chanan* is Strong's number 02603.

3. Christine Hoover, "What Does It Mean to Give Grace to One Another," *North American Mission Board*, June 16, 2016, accessed July 31, 2017, https://www.namb.net/flourish-blog/what-does-it-mean-to-give-grace-to-one-another.

4. Dale A. Robbins, "Beware of Satan's Secret Weapon!" *Victorious.org*, accessed July 7, 2017, http://www.victorious.org/pub/satans-weapon-unforgiveness-133.

5. Finis J. Dake, ed., *Dake's Annotated Reference Bible* (Lawrenceville, GA: Dake Publishing, 2014), s.v. *"makrothumia,"* NT 360.

Chapter 11: God's Love Covers

1. *Merriam-Webster Online Dictionary*, Merriam-Webster, 2015, s.v. "love."

2. Roman Krznaric, "The Ancient Greeks' 6 Words for Love (And Why Knowing Them Can Change Your Life)," *Yes! Magazine* online, December 27, 2013, accessed http://www.yesmagazine.org/happiness/the-ancient-greeks-6-words-for-love-and-why-knowing-them-can-change-your-life.

3. Ibid.

4. "Four Kinds of Love: Eros, Agape, Phileo, and Storge," *Eros to Agape*, August 9, 2012, accessed July 7, 2017, https://fromerostoagape.wordpress.com/2012/08/09/eros-romantic-love-and-agape-unconditional-love/.

5. Krznaric, "The Ancient Greeks' 6 Words for Love (And Why Knowing Them Can Change Your Life)," *Yes! Magazine* online, December 27, 2013.

6. Ibid.

7. "Four Kinds of Love: Eros, Agape, Phileo, and Storge," *Eros to Agape*, August 9, 2012.

8. Krznaric, "The Ancient Greeks' 6 Words for Love (And Why Knowing Them Can Change Your Life)."

9. Richard Savage, "Love Keeps No Record of Wrongs," *Active Christianity*, Brunstad Christian Church, accessed July 7, 2017, http://activechristianity.org/love-keeps-no-record-of-wrongs.

10. 10. Ibid.

Appendix: Biblical Truths on the Spirit of Bitterness

1. 1. The list of scriptures in this chapter have been excerpted from James Arendt, "Bible Topics: Bitterness," *Deep Truths,* accessed July 31, 2017, http://deeptruths.com/bible-topics/ bitterness.html.